Scraps of Life

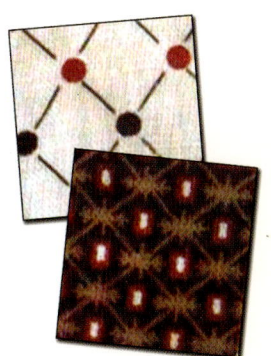

Author: Helen Ogden Widener

Photography and Graphics: Tad Browning

SCRAPS OF LIFE

Copyright© 2008
Helen Ogden Widener

Copyright© 2008
Photography and Graphics Designs
By Tad Alan Browning

All rights reserved. No part of this book may be reproduced, distributed or transmitted in any form or by any means including photocopy, mechanical or electronic productions without written permission from the Publisher, Pine Mountain Books. All images contained in the book are the copyright property of persons or archives who granted permission for their use.

Library of Congress Cataloging-in-Publication Data
Widener, Helen Ogden

Scraps of Life: Quilt top pieced 1850-1860 by Elizabeth Patton Crockett
Wife of Alamo Hero, David Crockett
A historical look at the life of Elizabeth Patton Crockett and
A step-by-step guide to creating her family heirloom.

ISBN: 978-0-615-26535-3

First Edition
Published by:
Pine Mountain Books
307 Steeplechase Drive
Irving, Texas 75062-3822
Email: hwidener@msn.com
Photography and Graphics:
Website: www.elizabethpattoncrockett.com

Printed in USA
by
Buzz Print, Dallas, Texas

Scraps of Life

Dedicated to

the memory of Elizabeth Patton Crockett

and her husbands

Pvt. James Patton,

Col. David Crockett

and all other servicemen and

women who have given us the

Gift of Freedom

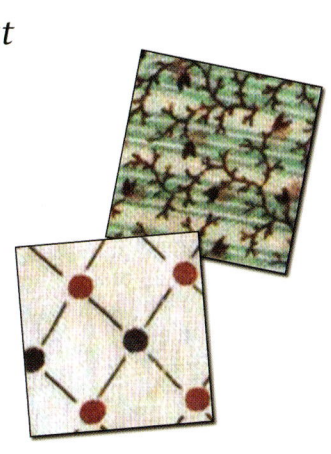

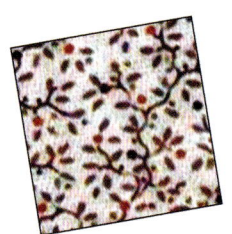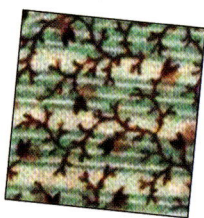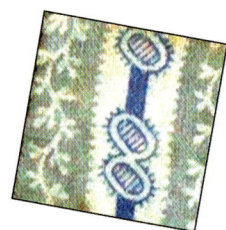

Contents

Frontier Woman   4

A Loving Gift   5

Introduction to Elizabeth Patton Crockett   6

History of Elizabeth Patton Crockett's Quilt Top   7

Elizabeth Patton Crockett's Original Quilt Top   8

Reproduction Quilt   9

Original Quilt Blocks and Antique Fabrics Gallery   10-70

Scraps of Life   11-69

Twenty-Four Dollar ($24) Payment   71

Elizabeth Patton Crockett Obituary   72

Elizabeth Crockett Monument   73

Scraps of Life Quilt Instructions   75

Acknowledgements   84

Special Contributors   85

Patton Family Genealogy   86

Patton-Crockett Family Genealogy   88

Crockett-Finley Family Genealogy   90

About the Author   93

Ambrotype Photo of Scottish Frontier Woman age 50-60, taken ca. 1850. Digitally enhanced and repaired. Facial features are similar to some Patton and Patton-Crockett descendants

Elizabeth Patton Crockett

There is always little time to put beauty into our lives, even though we crave beauty as much as any other women that ever lived. We sneak flowers among the garden vegetables. We take comfort and drink in the beauty and sound of our lyrical streams. We marvel at the fluffy white clouds in a wonder of blue. The green of the mountains reminds us of our supple and carefree youth. Never a moment passes that we do not find beauty hidden in the little recesses of the hardships of living.

It was soon after the death of The Colonel that my daughter-in-law, Rhoda, brought me her bag of pieces of material scraps. They were little pieces that had been carefully saved from the many dresses and shirts of our family. "Mother Betsy," she said, "Let's make a quilt." I had given little thought, for a very long time, to piecing a quilt. To be sure, my mother, Rebecca, had insisted that all her girls know every little thing about the keeping of a house and putting beauty in it. For the most part, my time had been spent running the mills, working around the house and in the garden. I oversaw the work of the younguns' and any hired help we might have had. The colors of my cabins had been, in part, left to chance. It was the neat little stacks of material that reminded me of the flowers and butterflies, the skies and our wonderful life giving earth. My mother had made many a quilt, many of which still brought us warmth at night and were creations of true beauty. During my years, I have done the hard work of a man, and still, it was a necessity that I teach the girls to sew and quilt, to keep house, cook the food and make the goods that we used in our everyday life.

These little pieces of material were the answer to my hurt and aching heart. A little something that could be put into a bag and easily carried along with my potions on the back of my horse. Sometimes the hours were long and lay heavy upon me while I was carin' for the sick, birthing a baby or tendin' a dying. It is during these times that we find God to be the strongest in our hearts. When counting our Blessings, we know the greatest of these are our children.

Scraps of Life Quilt Top, A loving gift made by

Elizabeth Patton Crockett

Introduction to Elizabeth Patton Crockett

Elizabeth was born May 22, 1788 in Swannanoa, Buncombe County, North Carolina. She was the fifth child of Robert Patton and Rebecca Cathey. Robert was a blacksmith and wagon maker whose shop was located on the old Bull Mountain Road that runs between Black Mountain and Rims Creek, North Carolina. Robert was very helpful in supplying wagons and wagon repairs during the American Revolution for which he received a large land grant.

The most difficult writing I faced in bringing this book to life, was how do I write about the life of a woman who had virtually nothing written about her? We know volumes about her famous husband, Col. David Crockett. Elizabeth was written about in terms of "my wife," and "I have an honest and industrious wife" or "she urged me to sell everything and do the right thing." Perhaps, the most profound insight into Elizabeth's character was found in David's letter to her brother, George Patton, written in Washington City on January 29, 1829, "I have been reproved many times for my wickedness by my Dear wife." This reference tells us that on occasion, she gave voice to her emotions and feelings.

Women of the 18th and 19th Century had no rights of ownership. Any possessions or inheritances, upon their marriage, became the property of their husband. In every aspect of the law women and all their possessions belonged to the men in their life. Little information can be gathered on most of the women who lived in that time period. However, through historical documents and the writings of their husbands, we see just how very important that women were to Frontier Life. The life of Elizabeth Patton Crockett speaks eloquently through the very essences of the absence of written words. The fabulous quilt top she left behind, tells us she had a heart filled with beauty, joy and artistic design. Based on historical documents, history of the time period, family background, and a writer's imagination and remembrance of my own Scots-Irish grandmother, I have tried to give a voice to Elizabeth as I feel she may have thought about life as it unfolded before her.

The 19th century woman's photograph used in this book, is an Ambrotype photograph taken of an unknown woman circa 1850. This is a true Frontier woman, who is dressed in widows black, a dress probably furnished by the photographer. She wears the snood that women of Scottish heritage wore. Her hands are those of a woman who did hard labor. The picture's look is one of a woman who has faced many hardships and her eyes say she has seen much sorrow. The facial features are consistent with some facial features of the George Patton family descendants. In keeping with Patton family descendents she was probably red headed, fair skinned with some freckles and a little taller than most women of the time period.

Helen Widener

The Elizabeth Patton Crockett "Quilt Top"

During the many years of Elizabeth's life she did what all Frontier women did, she saved all scraps of material from the families used clothing. From these scraps she pieced a very intricate "Quilt Top." All the blocks are the same block pattern. The fabrics in the quilt are different in each block. Another name for the pattern is "Postage Stamp" so named for the one inch squares that makes up all the blocks of the quilt top. The pattern was developed after the passing of a Congressional Bill to charge five cents to mail a letter. The top was never quilted, probably due to her death in 1860. The fabrics in the quilt top were all cotton and came from dressing gown, shirting and dress fabrics. The fabrics were used in clothing worn by all members of the family and included her sisters and their families as well. Many of the little blocks were cut through seam lines of the original garments making a pieced together one inch block. When friends, neighbors and family got together for a "Quilting Bee," they often exchanged bits of fabrics. Some of the fabric patterns were being made as early as the 1830s. Each block measures 12 x 12 inches. There are 2" connecting strips around the edge of the quilt and separating each of the blocks. The best description of the pattern might be "Postage Stamp Quilt on Point" as the blocks are laid out diagonally to form the diamond patterns. Each row of tiny blocks is artistically placed according to color and design to make a beautiful block. The arrangement of colors and designs are different.

The Quilt Top was given to Rhoda McWhorter Patton, wife of Elizabeth's son, George Patton. George and Rhoda had five sons and no daughters. The quilt top was handed down to granddaughter Rhoda Patton, the daughter of the oldest son, James Calvin Patton, who is the only descendant of George known to have had children, partly due to three brothers killed in the Civil War. The granddaughter, Rhoda, also did not have any daughters and gave the quilt top to Bernice Patton, the daughter of James' youngest son, Samuel Isaac Patton. Bernice married Stephen Vandermerwe. Bernice and Stephen were missionaries in South Africa for 50 years. The Quilt Top went back and forth to South Africa at least three times. The Quilt Top is now over 150 years old. In 1982, after the death of Bernice Patton Vandermerwe and at her request, the quilt top was donated to The Alamo. Because of its extremely fragile condition, the quilt top is no longer shown except under special circumstances and by appointment.

Tad Alan Browning, a military documentation photographer and graphic artist was given special permission by The Alamo to photograph and document the quilt top as well as each block individually. Tad is also a direct descendant of Elizabeth Patton Crockett through her son, George Patton.

*This "Postage Stamp on Point" Quilt Top of scraps
was made by Elizabeth Patton Crockett prior to her death in 1860.
The Quilt Top was handed down through the family of
Elizabeth's son, George Patton. Elizabeth was the widow
of Alamo Hero, Col. David Crockett*

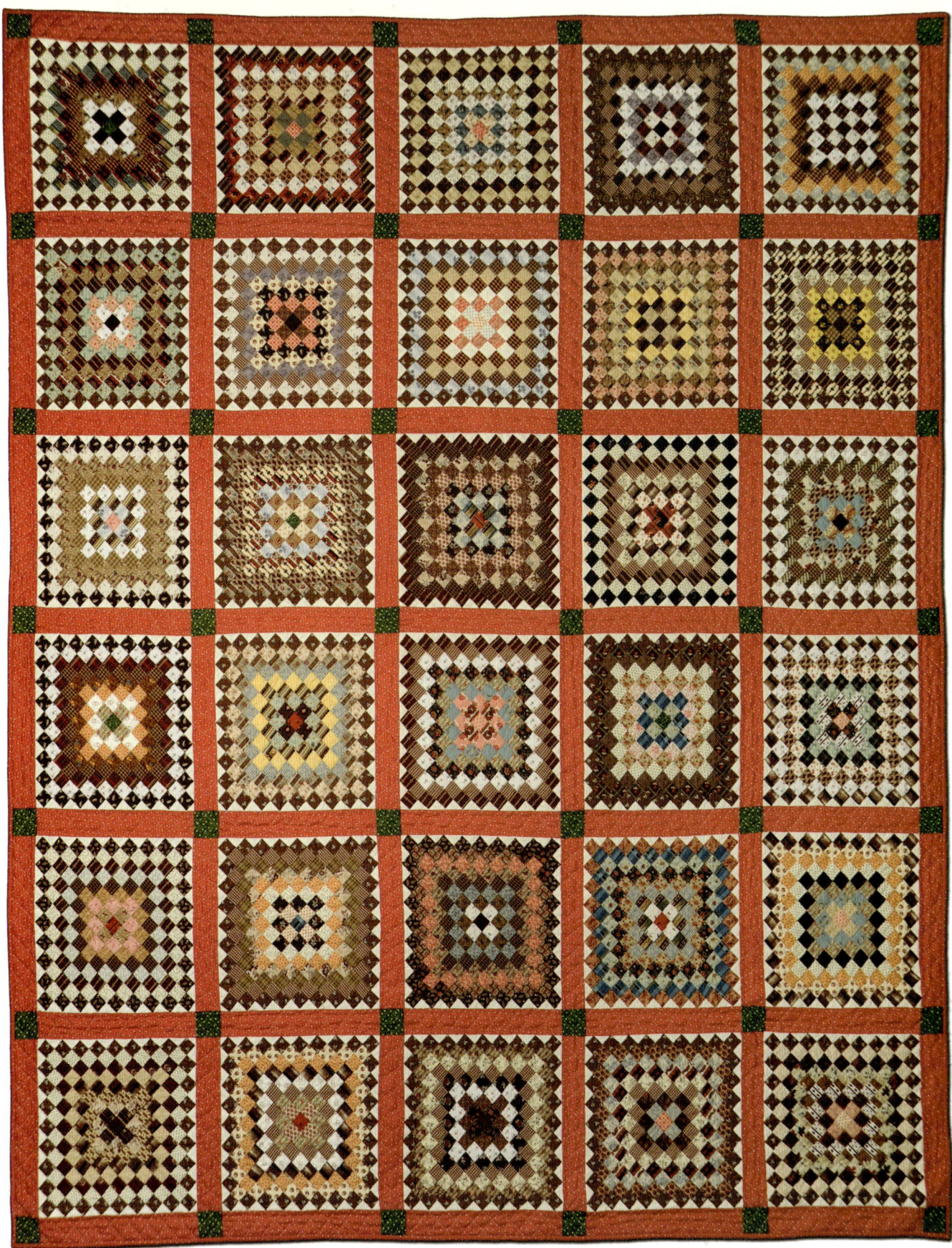

Reproduction –Scraps of Life
Postage Stamp on Point Quilt
Pieced by Helen Ogden Widener - 2008

Antique Fabrics Gallery

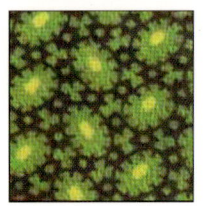   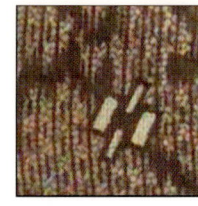 
  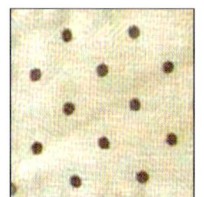  

Charge of the Frontiersmen- American Revolution, Battle of Kings Mountain took place on 7 October 1780 in York County South Carolina near the North Carolina Border.

Image courtesy of the New York Public Library

1780 September – The Patton Brothers, Burke Co. North Carolina

Robert and Elijah Patton worked hard tending their forge and building wagons to help replace those lost during the Battle of Camden. British "Bloody Ban" Tarletan had destroyed the wagons, cannons and rifles and slaughtered most of the men of the Southern forces. The Pattons would contribute as many wagons and goods as they had. A near neighbor, Mary McKeehan Patton contributed 500 pounds of gun powder to the Overmountain Men on their way to the Battle of Kings Mountain.

Both brothers were in awe of General George Washington and his brave war efforts through unimaginable hardships. Having come from Ireland in their youth, they both were aware of the consequence for the losers of a war. The English would take no pity on any who had helped with goods and services for the revolution, just as they had taken no prisoners in the Battle of Culloden of 1746. Due to that battle, the people of Scotland lost their Sovereignty and were now under the devastating control of England's King George. With horror, the brothers imagined the English shouted orders of "No Quarter." England forced the Patton family out of Scotland into Northern Ireland where the brothers were born. Their father, John Patton, had brought his sons including their brothers, John and Samuel Patton to the Colonies for a better life. They had migrated from their arrival place in Pennsylvania and followed the Appalachian Mountain Ridges to their present place of residence in North Carolina.

The script or receipt for goods, received by Robert and Elijah became land grants after America won the war and became a nation. A near neighbor, George Cathey had several daughters. Robert married Rebecca Cathey and his brother Elijah married her sister, Margaret. There were more marriages in coming years between the Patton-Cathey cousins.

Author's Note:
The Revolutionaries won the day at King's Mountain, smashed the English forces saving the South and saving the Revolution.

Antique Fabrics Gallery

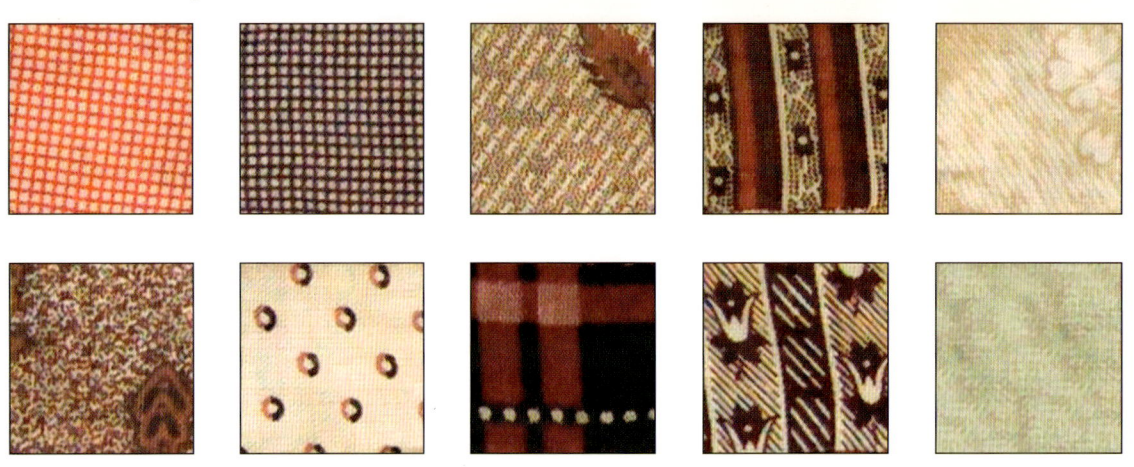

The Patton brothers were blacksmiths and wagon makers and were adept at carpentry and iron work. The 19th century forge was brought from Northern Ireland.

Image courtesy of Mike Sutton of the Virginia Cultural Museum, Staunton, Va. Russ Stallings is at the forge.

May 22, 1788 Swannanoa, North Carolina - Birth of Elizabeth Patton

Two sisters, Rebecca and Margaret Patton, worked together to bring Rebecca's fifth child into the world. The beautiful Swannanoa valley and the lovely May weather allowed Mary Burgin, another sister, to take the older children, away from the house, into the woods to gather berries and wild greens. She promised the children a special treat of Blackberry Cobbler.

Both sisters had played the goodwife for each other during their times of lying in. They each knew the use of the special herbs, which grew in the mountains that lessened the birthing dangers and eased the pain. Herbs were always gathered and dried during the summer months to preserve the strength of the herb.

Robert was busy at his forge, and the sisters could hear the repeated hammer of iron against iron with echoes across the valley. Sometimes, they could hear the hiss of the heated metal being plunged into cold water. Between the clangs of metal against metal, birds supplied their magical tunes to ease the long birthing process. Trees were clothed in new green leafed coats and flowers raised their beautiful colorful faces toward the sun. The sisters could hear all the familiar sounds drifting through the open window. All was well with the family, and there would be much to celebrate following the safe arrival of the child.

The children returned to find the bed curtain pulled open, so they could see the new baby. Names for the baby girl flowed rapidly from tiny lips. It was Margaret's two year old son James, who would lisp out the name of Elizabeth for the tiny baby girl. Elizabeth Patton, called "Betsy" became the newest "redheaded" addition to the Patton Clan.

Author's Note:
A typical scene of a Frontier woman birthing a child might have been something like this. Midwifes or healing women were also known as goodwives in Scotland.

Antique Fabrics Gallery

Chopping trees and getting the logs ready to build a cabin was a powerful lot of work, and cooking over an open fire for all those who were working and tending a small child at the same time, was pretty hard work too.

Building a new farm

Spring 1809 – The Wedding at Swannanoa

I married my cousin, James Patton. James was the best friend of my brother, George as they were the same age. All the teasing endured during the "growing up" years was now past. Our marriage was performed at the Patton Meeting House, which was used for Worship and any Social gatherings for our Scots-Irish Presbyterian family, as well as the surrounding community. Papa built the Meeting House himself, to ensure that his family had a place to keep our religious faith. Family worship, marriages and christenings were the foundation of our family. It would remain so for many generations to come.

After the wedding ceremony, we all danced to the tunes of our beloved bagpipes, fiddles and harps. We also had competition games such as being the best shot with a rifle and a favorite game of "pitching horseshoes" to fall around a peg placed in the ground.

Our community gathered for weddings during the summer months, when the roads were less muddy and rutted. People came from far and wide to attend any important social occasion bringing pickled and spiced meats, home preserved vegetables, mince pies and cakes to share with all who came. People cooked in the open and slept around their wagons, packed with quilts for the families' comfort and for the communities' admiration.

Our neighbor women pooled their resources to make my Wedding Cake. It took four pounds of extra fine flour, two-dozen eggs, three pounds of butter and three pounds of sugar. Raisins, molasses and spices and a quantity of brandy completed the Cake. The brandy preserved the cake, which took several days to make. The cake was large enough for everyone to enjoy.

Author's Note:
James was the son of Elizabeth's uncle Elijah Patton and aunt Margaret Cathey Patton who lived in Burke County, North Carolina.

Antique Fabrics Gallery

Log Cabin Quilt made by Pearl Rivers(Masters) Walker ca. 1930-40. Quilt owned by Isabel Gravle of Frankston, Texas

1810 - Moving to Franklin County, Tennessee

My new husband and I lived for a time in Burke County near his parents on the Catawba River. Uncle Elijah had taken his Revolutionary Land Grant in Franklin County, in the State of Tennessee where we were going to make our home. It took until the end of the summer for the men of the family to build the farmstead where James and I would move with our new baby son, George, who arrived in the spring.

Our cousins, Ann Gillespie and husband Robert and their families, moved to Franklin with James and me. There was a considerable collection of relatives moving along down the mountain. Traveling and living together was necessary for protection from Indians and mishaps along the way. It also provided us help and fellowship with each other. Cooking and caring for the camp was for the women and physical work and hunting for the men.

Our families arrived to the newly built cabins and, with few belongings, settling in took a very short time. There were crops ready to harvest and pack away for the coming winter. We women milked the cows, made butter and preserved the meats. We kept the fires in the cook house going to feed our families and travelers that were always passing by.

The farm was prosperous and had a mill for the grinding of grains as well as James' blacksmith shop which provided services and income for our family and small community. Things did not stay peaceful as incidents with renegade Indians had increased in alarming numbers. The Indians were being encouraged by the English, with the help of strong spirits, to wage war against the settlers. The English had not accepted the fact that the Colonies were lost to them forever.

Author's Note:
Ann Gillespie was a cousin of Elizabeth through the Cathey Family. During the many years of Elizabeth's life, she would have her family around her providing support, comfort and always companionship.

Antique Fabrics Gallery

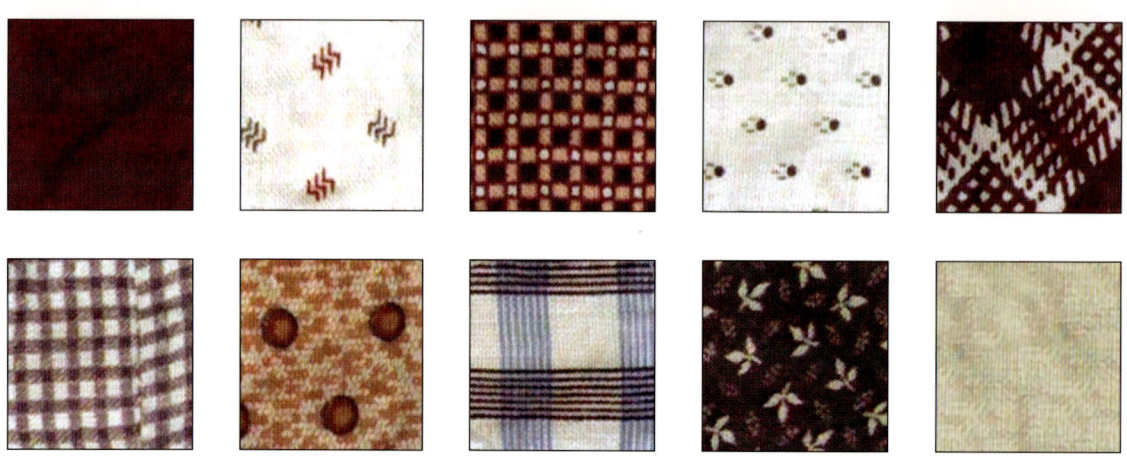

The massacre at Fort Mims occurred on August 30, 1813 when the Creek Indians, called "Red Sticks", overran the fort killing 517 settlers and militia-men

The Battle of Fort Mims - Image courtesy of New York Public Library

1813 - James Patton goes to War

It was the early part of September in 1813 when we received the news at Spring Cove Creek of the terrible bloody massacre at Fort Mims.

In the first days of October, James left me with the care of our small son and daughter. He saddled his horse and rode to Winchester. James signed up with Captain William Russell's company who was in charge of General Andrew Jackson's military spies. We had only enough time to get his supplies together and say goodbye.

Time passed slowly even with the daily chores to be done. All the crops were stored away before James left. I pickled barrels of meats, some sauerkraut and stored mounds of potatoes in the ground to keep them from freezing. We had plenty of corn hominy for grits. Sugar and salt cured hams were hanging in the smoke house. Our larder was full. I spent my lonely nights before the fire, piecing a quilt, making garments or repairing those things we used every day.

From time to time men hunting in the area would drop in to have a bite to eat and exchange news of the war. We learned there was terrible fighting in Alabama. Our men, enraged over the deaths of our innocents, set fire to one of the Indian Villages where some of the renegade Indian braves had run to hide. Our men burned the village and shot all that lived there. It was the same type of killing that their people did at Fort Mims. It made me ill to think about the terrible slaughter and loss of life.

Just before Christmas we received a visit from Mr. Crockett, a neighbor who lived over on Bean Creek. It was a surprise, as I knew he was also fighting the Creeks.

Author's Note:
After the attack on Fort Mims, settlers in the area were terrified. Most of the men would sign up to fight for a given number of days as they were leaving women and children unprotected and alone in a dangerous Frontier environment. Instead of a civil war between Indians it was now a war between the Indians and the United States.

Antique Fabrics Gallery

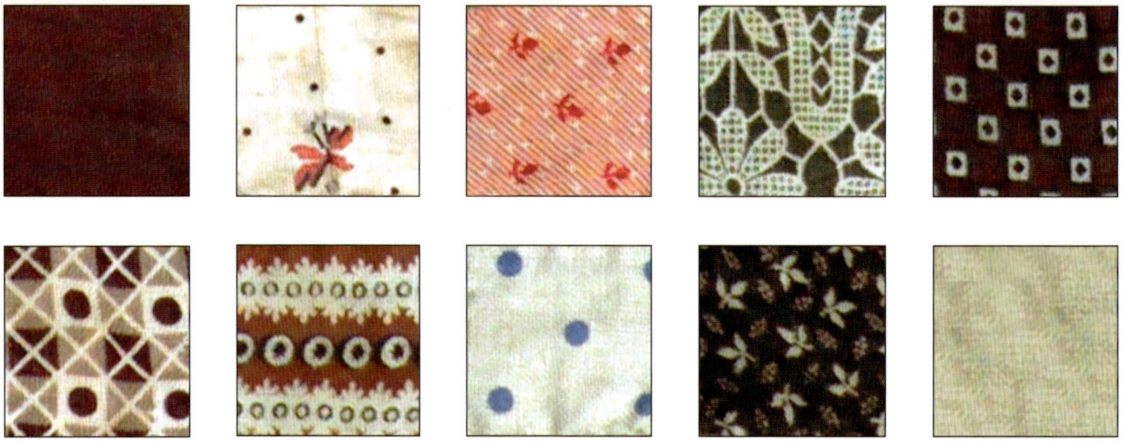

  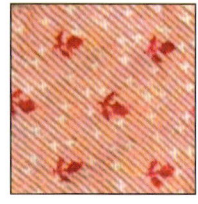  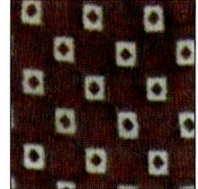
  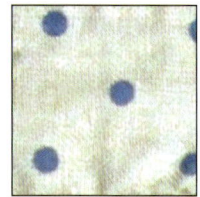  

The Battle of Talladega was fought November 9th, 1813 between the Red Stick Creek Indians and the Tennessee Militia near the Coosa River in Alabama.

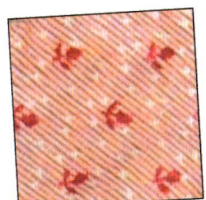

Battle of Talladega - Image courtesy of New York Public Library

1813 – November 23, Death of James Patton

It was the sad look on Mr. David Crockett's face, rather than his words, that told me of my husband's death. The little ones were clingin' to my skirts, but I asked him to come on in the cabin. He slid off his horse, took a deer from behind and laid it out on the porch. Food in times of grievin' brings comfort.

I reckon there weren't words that could come from my mouth. Mr. Crockett understood and began his tale of horror. On the 7th of November, he said, we had seen fighting at Big Warrior Town and after the battle we were all hungry and took what food we could find. We later came upon a herd of wild hogs that gave us meat for some days. We crossed over the Coosa River and headed to the fort. On the 9th, we had only just arrived when Capt. Russell and his men began making their way around the fort. The friendly Indians inside the fort began to call and point to the river. The men made a run for the fort but some took arrows on the way. There were hordes of savages coming over the banks of the river with hatchets out and arrows already in the air. The Indians were terrible in their look, painted scarlet, and naked as the day they were born. Our bullets were like swarms of hornets flying into that mess of painted flesh. We lost 15 of our men in the fight. We put the wounded on litters made of hides to carry them back to Fort Strother where your husband and my friend died.

My heart and mind were too shattered and numb to hear more. I gathered my children to me and watched Mr. Crockett as he disappeared into the forest.

Author's Note:
The battle described, was the Battle of Talladega. James died of his wounds on November 23, 1813 while at Fort Strother. Fort Strother was located near the present day town of Ohatchee, Alabama.

Antique Fabrics Gallery

Swannanoa Presbyterian Church. The first church built to replace the Old Patton Meeting House. The church has been rebuilt and enlarged several times. Photo by Helen Widener

First Presbyterian Church of Swannanoa, North Carolina

1815 July – Going Home to Swannanoa

When a mighty oak falls, the groans and shattering of its trunk disrupts everything around it. The little animals and birds, who called it home, will leave and find another. The falling of a loved one leaves a shattered heart that cries silently in its grief. It makes no sound but brings the feeling of devastation and loss as that of the mighty oak.

It had now been two lonely winters with my children, George now age 5 and Margaret age 4, since the loss of my husband, James. It was late in July, and I was making preparations for a trip to North Carolina to see my folks as was usual this time of the year. We would stay through the month of August and return in time to put away the crops and prepare for the winter. I hadn't a fear of things going wrong, as the Gillispies were always near. We were, in the early hours of the morning, packing the horses for our trip, when to my surprise, I saw my neighbor, Mr. David Crockett coming through the trees.

As he came through the trees, he paused, looked around, and continued on to the front porch. He had accompanied me to a few frolics and we knew each other. He asked if we were leaving for a spell. I told him "yes" we were heading up the wagon road into North Carolina to see my family. He rather casually remarked that he had thought to go along that way himself. I readily invited him to come along with us, as it was safer for more people to travel together.

Soon after the death of his wife Polly, Mr. Crockett's brother and family had come to live with him and help with the care of his three small children.

Author's Note:
There is only speculation as to the actual events that took place when David Crockett came acourtin' the widow. There is also speculation that it took some persuasion for Elizabeth to marry David Crockett. However, David needed a wife and "sly as a fox," he set out to make a bargain.

Antique Fabrics Gallery

Young David Crockett in Hunting dress. This picture is probably close to what David looked like when he married Elizabeth. He had dark hair, blue eyes and a "rosy" complexion and was about 6 feet tall.

1815 August – The Handfast Bargain

By the time we reached North Carolina, I could tell Mr. Crockett was aimin' for a marriage. Little Polly, his wife, had died only three months before. I knew the grief that his children must feel. On the frontier, we all did the best we could. It was especially difficult for a man or woman not to have the comfort and help of a spouse. By the time we reached the cabin of my parents we were comfortable in the presence of the other, and he won the hearts of my children. Little George and Margaret missed the story telling and the good nature of a loving father.

Papa and Momma were happy to see our little family but were somewhat suspicious of the gentleman who traveled with us. However, it was easy for them to see that we had grown fond of each other. We spoke of marriage but the Circuit Judge had already gone for the winter. David, always one to be quick with a word or solution to a problem suggested that we have a "Handfast Marriage." It was an old fashioned practice of immigrants of Celtic Heritage. Papa consented and would hear our oaths, tie the tartan around our hands, and be our witness. The marriage was legal in the same way as a marriage before a minister or magistrate. It was a bargain for one year and one day. Should I conceive a child of the union, the marriage would become permanent and when the Circuit Judge came around next spring we would have a Civil Marriage ceremony complete with a celebration with our families and friends.

On returning home, David and his three children moved into my cabin.

Author's Note:
According to some Patton Family Histories, David and Elizabeth were married in August of 1815. Celtic style Handfast marriages were still fairly common in the Appalachian Mountains through the middle of the 20th Century, with many couples never going through a civil ceremony.

Antique Fabrics Gallery

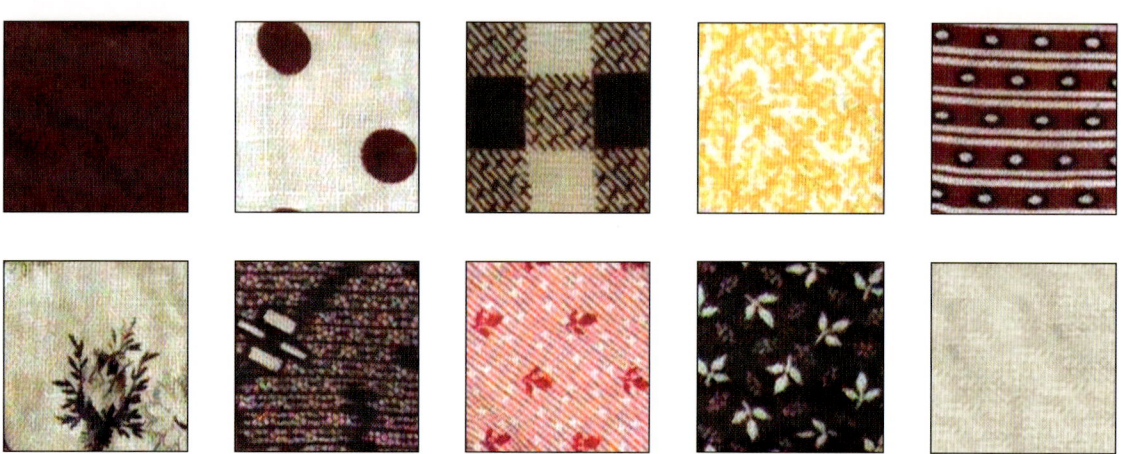

Double Wedding Ring Quilt made by Madeline Dunklin of Frankston, Texas. Photo courtesy of Larry and Sherry Dunklin

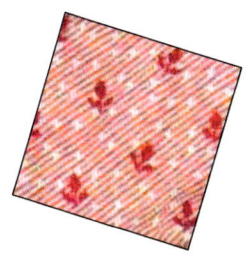

Spring 1816 - the Magistrate comes

The snows had receded, and the roads were now busy with the comings and goings of spring. Richard Calloway, our community magistrate, was now in the area, so David and I made our announcements and invited all our families and neighbors to a wedding that would take place on Saturday. A person had to get married when the magistrate was in the area. For a few months he was very busy.

Our guests sat all around the cabin and some outside. Before I could come from the other room, where I had put on my best dress, I heard a commotion with lots of laughter and giggling. Peeking around the door, I saw the funniest sight. Our old pet pig, Hook, had wandered in through the cabin door giving a most entertaining show. Old Hook was grunting around all the folks. David, all calm and solemn took Old Hook by the ear and led him outside. With a sheepish grin he said, "Old Hook from now on, I'll do the grunting around here." I waited until all was quiet and then opened the door and joined my husband-to-be in front of our magistrate.

In a few days our world settled down, and in September I gave birth to our first child, Robert Patton Crockett. Following our son's birth, David with three of our neighbors, Robinson, Frazier and Rich set out for the Creek Country to look for new lands. We learned our cozy little farm still belonged to my former father-in-law, Elijah Patton and he was unwilling for us to continue farming the land which my late husband, James and I worked so hard to build. Knowing that women could not own land, Uncle Elijah kept the farm, intended for James, for his grandchildren.

Author's Note:
An article of an old Nashville newspaper of the 1930s, gave the story of the wedding as related by Mrs. Katherine Kelly who remembered her great-grandfather, Richard Calloway performing the ceremony in May 1816.

Antique Fabrics Gallery

There were many remedies used during the Frontier days, as that was all the people knew to do. Used were Opium and alcohol for internal complaints and for skin injuries pine tar (like present day black ointment) was frequently used to draw out impurities. Photo by Tad Browning.

1816 Fall – David's near death

After a couple of weeks, when David had not returned, I began to worry. Our neighbors returned without my husband, bringing his horse and the news that David had died. For several days I was in such a state, I could do nothing. Finally, I hired a man to try to find where David had died and to recover his personal property.

Before the man could return my poor husband reappeared. He had been terribly sick and looked to be half dead, but thankfully was still alive.

After rest and food, we gathered around to hear his story.

"Well," he said, "When I heard I was dead, I knew that was a real whopper." He continued his story. "After we left, our horses got loose and I went after them to bring them back. I must have traveled on foot for over 50 miles, wading creeks and swamps and climbing hills and mountains. By night fall, I still had not caught them and knew that I would not. Remembering a house I had passed, I returned there for the night. The next morning, when I woke up, I was so sore and fatigued that I didn't think that I could walk anymore. Being anxious to return to my company, I set out back the way that I had come. By noon, I had such a headache I knew I could go no further. I sat down beside the trace, and prepared to wait until I was feeling better. Some Indians came along and offered me melons to eat but I was too sick. The Indians helped me to a house where I stayed. The woman gave me a whole bottle of Bateman's Drops, which I thought would kill me, but made me well."

Author's Note:
The story comes from the Autobiography of David Crockett by David Crockett. Bateman's Drops were primarily 49% alcohol with 2 grams of Opium. Other ingredients are not listed on the box.

Antique Fabrics Gallery

*The Crockett Gristmill stood on the bank of Shoal Creek in Lawrence County, Tennessee.
Photo by Helen Widener*

1817 Spring – Lawrence County, Tennessee

With rest and good food, my husband soon regained the strength to resume the duties of providing food and comfort for our family. I hoped that I would never again hear of his death.

In the spring, David was determined to find us a new place to live. This place, he thought, was a sickly place, and if we wanted to raise a healthy family we needed to move. David had heard of an area about 80 miles away that sounded good. It was known as Shoal Creek. He left to take a look around and was gone for about three months. I had begun to worry, but knew he was to build us a cabin before he returned. He again became sick, but by the time he recovered he had become pleased with the place and decided to settle there. He put up a cabin and returned for our six children and me. We packed all our goods, settled the children into the oxen drawn wagon, and in less than two weeks were pulling up to our wonderful new cabin.

There was no law and order in the community. A group got together to form something of a government and David was appointed as one of the magistrates. It was a hard task making out warrants to people who didn't pay their bills or stole from others. At the time my husband was a poor hand at writing so found it difficult to write out the warrant. In a short while his writing improved and the job became an easier one. He also, now by law, became an Esquire. How proud I was to have such a husband and happy were his children to call him Papa.

Author's Note:
The move to Shoal Creek started the rise of David's political career and a prosperous family life. With the construction of a Grist Mill, the family ground corn, made gunpowder and distilled whiskey. It was a good time of life for Elizabeth and David Crockett.

Antique Fabrics Gallery

The original quilt made by Mrs. H.E. Thomas in 1949 consisted of 48 states. She redesigned and remade the quilt after the addition of two more states to make the quilt a fifty state quilt. The blocks were re-cut, changing them from square to hexagon. Courtesy of Ben and Bobbie Thomas of Irving, Texas

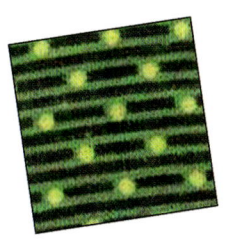

1818 Fall - Captain Matthews' Frolic

We settled into our new home, planting a big garden and plenty of corn. I kept the girls in the cabin helping with the baking, candle making and spinning. Before the beginning of fall, I knew our family would be expanding. Our home was warm and cozy and another child would be a blessing. I was now thirty years old, a woman of some maturity.

One morning one of our neighbors, a Captain Matthews came to call on David. He told David he was running for the position of Colonel for a regiment. My husband had become a man of means and importance. He wanted David's support and for him to run for the position of First Major. David had done a lot of fighting and was not in such a way as to want to do anymore. At the insistence and persuasion of Matthews, David finally relented and consented to go for the position.

All our family attended Captain Matthews' big frolic, with electioneering, food and a chance to visit with our neighbors. Any frolic brought out a crowd, and this one was no exception. I happened to hear that Captain Matthews' son was running against my husband and quickly related the unwelcome news to him.

It was a real blow to David to learn Captain Matthews had played him false. It really got his dander up and he decided to call out the Captain and find out for himself the cause of the falsehood. Captain Matthews admitted that his son was also running for First Major, but otherwise he said, he would gladly vote for David. David informed Captain Matthews that he had decided not to run for First Major but to run for the position of Colonel of the regiment. He would be running against Captain Matthews and not the Captain's son.

Author's Note:
Electioneering was another reason for all the area to come together for visiting and catching up on what was happening in the community. Most of the people lived in areas that were not close to neighbors. A frolic for any reason was an exciting occasion.

Antique Fabrics Gallery

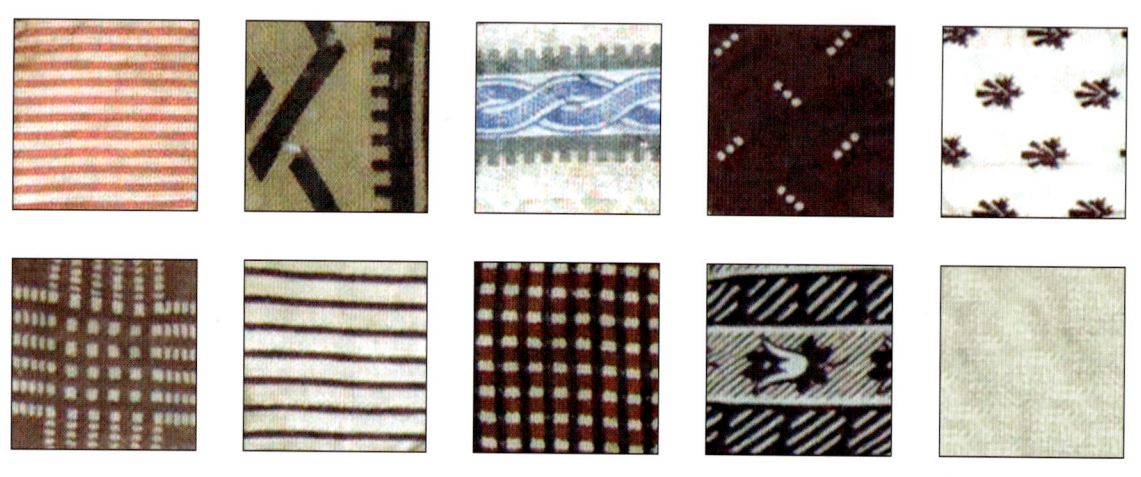

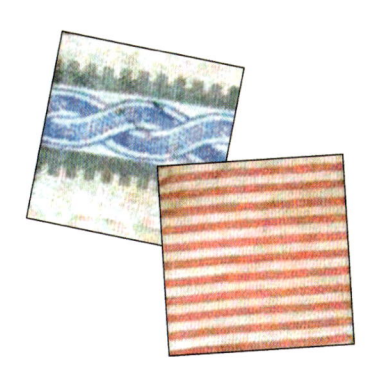

1840-50s Pennsylvania style Cradle with early Sunbonnet Sue quilt owned by Rebecca Power. Photo by Tad Browning

Fall 1818 - The New Colonel

By the time the election was over and the votes counted, David had become the new Colonel. He explained to the crowd that he had changed his mind about running for First Major as Captain Matthews' own son was running for the same position. David's comments were that he guessed since he was running against the whole family he would take on the "head of the mess."

Our standing in the community had taken a great rise, and our grist mill was bringing in a substantial income for us. We had a man who ran the mill, but it was a job in which all the family took part. I packed and stacked many sacks of cornmeal as well as helped with the distillery and the making of gun powder which we sold.

Shoal Creek was a beautiful place to live with a little falls that turned the stone grinding wheels. We had gone deeply in debt to buy the wheels, but the success of our business would pay off the loans. The mill was sitting by the creek with a trough that brought water pouring over the wheel that turned the grindings stones to grind the grains. We made wonderfully fine cornmeal and flour. A more beautiful and peaceful place to live, could not be found on the face of the earth. Our porch, overlooking the creek, provided us with many evenings of peace and pleasure. I sewed and knitted until the light was too dim for me to see. Then, I would go into the house and prepare our evening meal. I sometimes cooked our meal to the tunes of David's violin and the happy play of the children. December 25, 1818, I gave birth to Rebecca Elvira Crockett.

Author's Note:
Elizabeth spent most of her time in the home. Doing hard work in the mill and garden during the day and enjoying the evenings with her family. She sewed dresses for the girls and shirts for the boys or sat quietly mending or piecing a quilt.

Antique Fabrics Gallery

Crockett Violin – According to legend, Davy Crockett played this violin the night before the Battle of The Alamo.

Image courtesy of Witte Museum, San Antonio, Texas

1821 – Tennessee State Legislature

Our life proceeded with speed, as we had now been married for five years. The Colonel, as I now referred to my husband, was induced to run for the Tennessee State Legislature, which he won. The speech he gave during his campaign was quite remarkable. All the community had gathered for a frolic and some electioneering. Before the frolic, the men chose up teams to go for a squirrel hunt. The Colonel shot a good many squirrels, and his side was the winner.

Before the dancing began, the candidates for office gave their speeches. A long winded bunch of men would have been hard to surpass. The Colonel got up to give his speech and told everyone they knew what he was there for, to get their votes and if they weren't careful, he would get them too. He said he had a whole passel of words to say but couldn't get them up. He told a story about a man who was trying to open a barrel that he knew contained whiskey. However, he wasn't able to get the barrel open. He was like that man he said, he knew the words were there but he just couldn't get them to come out. After a couple of short stories that had the gathering laughing, The Colonel said he had a throat so dry, he reckoned he couldn't choke up any more words and didn't believe there was a man out there who was not as dry as he was. He invited the men to join him at the drink barrel and have a horn to wet their throats. Most of the men joined him, leaving the remaining speakers to speak to the remaining few, who were interested enough to listen.

It was not long before The Colonel picked up his violin and began a fast paced fiddlin' meaning there would be no more speeches today.

Author's Note:
Colonel David was a popular man welcomed for his backwoods humor and his common bond with the people in his district.

Antique Fabrics Gallery

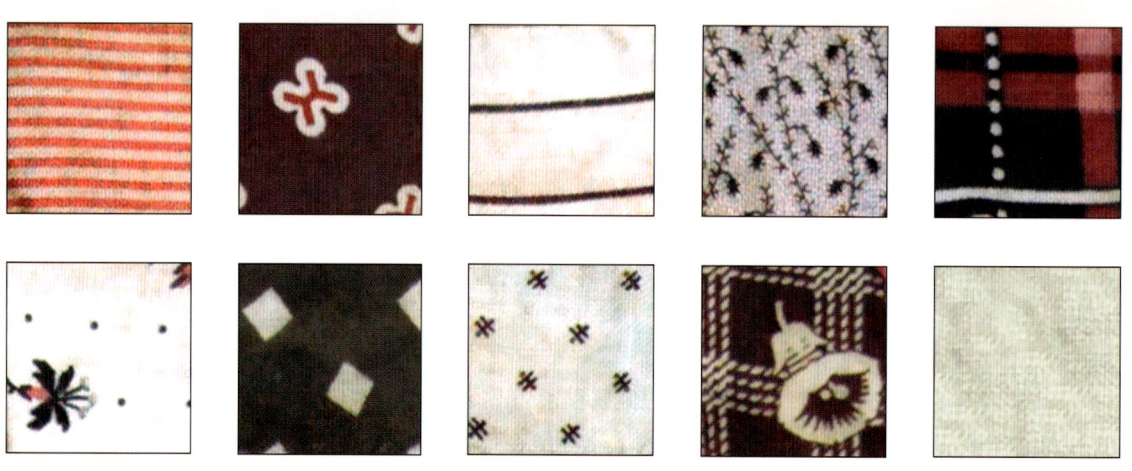

Old mill of Tennessee. The Grist Mill owned by David Crockett may have looked something like this. Photo courtesy of Tennessee Library and Archives.

1821 Spring – The Big Fresh

The Colonel packed his new white shirts and new wool trousers and left to go to the State House for his first Session of the Legislature. He would be there for three months.

This time of year was mighty busy, with the hunting to refresh our meat supplies, planting the garden and putting in the crops. Some of the needed items were drinking spirits and gun powder. It was also a time of melting snows and lots of rain. Our creeks were running so full as to threaten to overrun their banks.

We could see heavy clouds late one evening. The rain would come but our cabin was well above the creek. I went to bed knowing all our family was safe and snug in our beds. Before morning, the roar of water coming down the river awakened me. By the sounds I was hearing, I knew our grist mill was under attack. The big fresh swept away our grist mill and our source of good income.

John Wesley took the horse and started out for the State House to fetch The Colonel and bring him home. He arrived to find an empty place on the banks of Shoal Creek where our grist mill had stood. Standing it its place was a whole passel of busted dreams and a pocketful of debts. There was nothing left to salvage. Our grinding stones were buried somewhere beneath the sands of the river and were nowhere to be found. It was a trying time for our family.

On August Second of 1821, a hot and sultry day, our third child, Matilda Crockett was born. Our family now consisted of eight children. I was thirty-three years of age and the children I now had, were blessings enough.

Author's Note:
Hard work and a dedicated effort to get ahead and take care of a family was hard and uncertain on the frontier proved by David's many narrow escapes from death and the many unlucky happenings that came his way.

Antique Fabrics Gallery

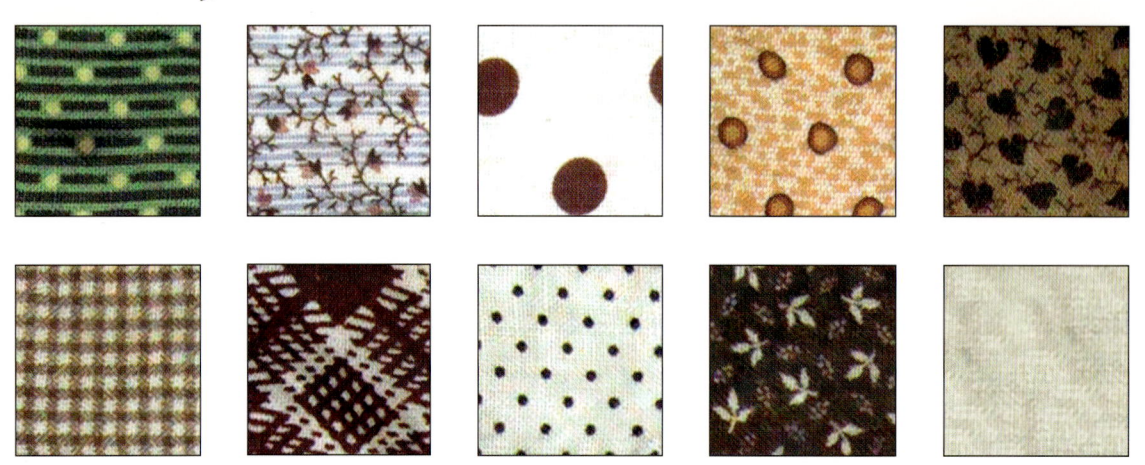

*David Crockett was a well known bear hunter and was believed to be his favorite sport. This bear rug hangs in the old Crockett Cabin in Rutherford, Tennessee.
Photo by Helen Widener*

1822 Summer - Move to Obion River, Gibson County

After the destruction of the mill there was nothing to do but sell everything in hopes of starting again.

The Colonel was that worried. He wanted to know what we were going to do, with everything gone and debts more than we could pay. I told him we had to "do the right thing, sell the farm, sell everything and we would scuffle along." It was the very thing he wanted to hear as he had an aversion to unpaid debts. I remembered Papa had a Thousand acres of land from his service to the Revolution over on the Obion River.

The Colonel left, taking his son, John Wesley and a young man by the name of Abram Henry with him to finish his term in the Legislature and then to go on to the Obion and try to locate Papa's land. A better Papa a woman or man never had; he agreed to deed 800 acres of the land to the Colonel. It was plenty enough for a "brand-fire" new start.

On the trip, John Wesley became so chilled the Colonel had to leave him and Abram with a family who lived near the acres where the Colonel would build our cabin. By the time he built the cabin he had run out of gun powder. The river was flooded and in such a rage that crossing it, almost cost him his life. However, he secured the powder, killed a buck, hung it from a tree, dressed it out, took some of the meat and headed back to the newly built cabin. He was in such a bad state of fatigue, that he could barely bring himself to eat enough of the deer, he had killed, to restore his strength. As soon as the river subsided he picked up the boys. They put in the crops and headed back home for the rest of the family.

Author's Note:
By the time of this incident, David had become a widespread legend for his hunting ability and the physical strength to overcome anything that might come his way.

Antique Fabrics Gallery

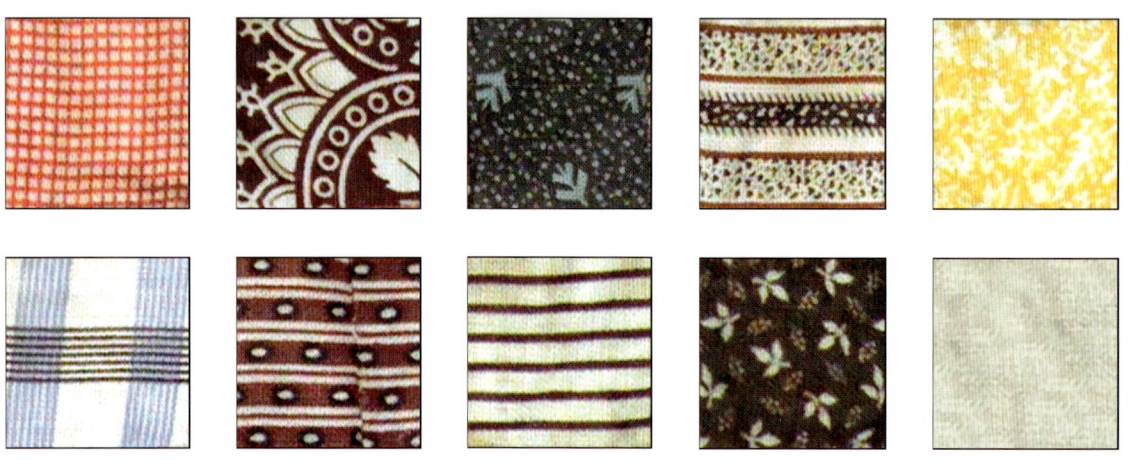

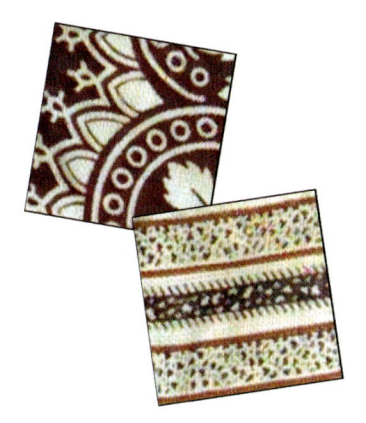

Tennessee Black Bear – photo courtesy of Tennessee Library and Archives

1825 Fall - The Big Bear Hunt

Our family was now well settled in our new cabin on Obion River in the county of Gibson. The Colonel had finished his term in the Legislature and been asked to run for Congressman for the State of Tennessee.

The Colonel campaigned all through the summer months only to lose his bid for the Congressional Seat. He was somewhat disheartened by the loss and decided to go bear hunting. Bear hides, as well as bear fat and meat was a ready source of income. During the length of that year the Colonel killed 105 of Tennessee's abundant population of black bears. At least two of them weighed more than 600 pounds.

The trail traveled by the Colonel was marked to show the direction he was traveling. The boys followed behind with a horse and sled to skin, cut up the bears and haul them back to the cabin where the hard work really began. The hide had to be tanned, the fat removed and the meat cut into smaller pieces. I had the fire going all day around the clock and the old black pot bubblin' over the fire to render out the bear fat. We packed most of the fat into barrels to sell, some I used to make lye soap and some softer soap scented with wild honeysuckle which we cut, wrapped into bars and also sold. We preserved some of the meat in brine and spices and sold that too. It was a winter of very hard work and an abundance of food. Bear was not all that the Colonel hunted; he killed any creatures that were good for food. We had fried squirrel, deer and plenty of pork. We sometimes had turkey, duck or goose.

Author's Note:
The abundance of food in the nearly unsettled country in which the Crockett's moved provided most of the food that the family needed. Coats, clothing, moccasins and bed covers were made from hides. The animal's sinew was used in sewing together the leather clothing as it was stronger.

43

Antique Fabrics Gallery

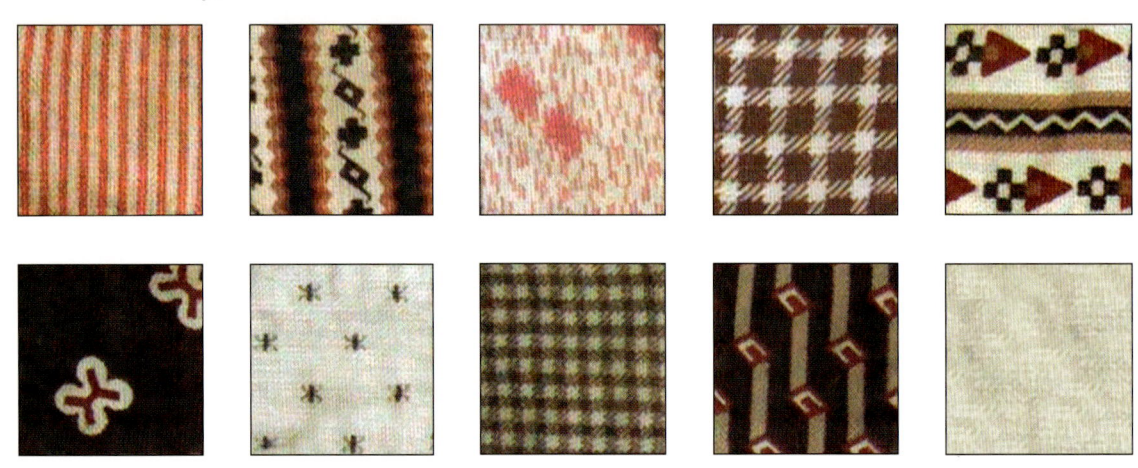

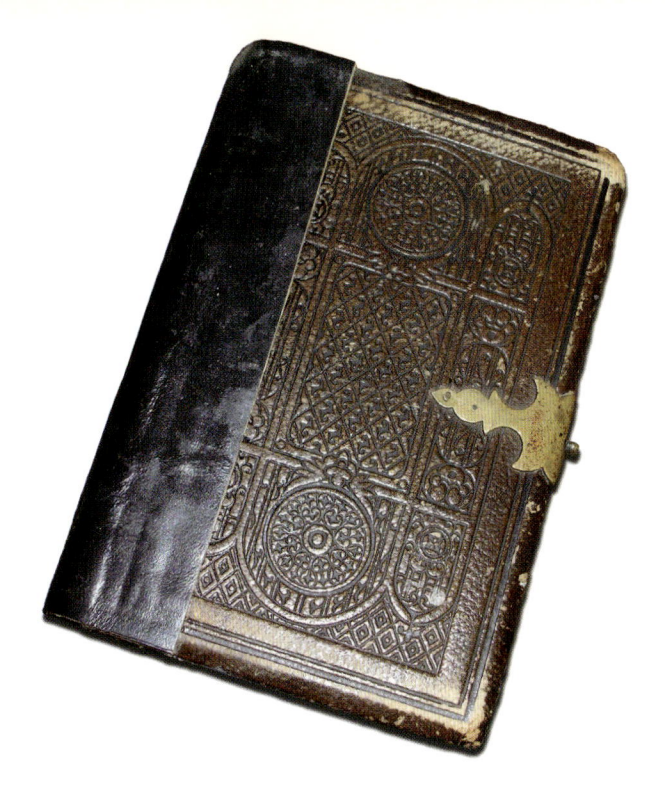

1850s Prayer book - With the constant threat to life during the frontier years, a prayer book in hand was a great comfort to wives whose husbands were away from home. Photo by Helen Widener.

1826 – The making of barrel staves

The older boys, John, William and George were now big strapping young men adept at felling trees, chopping and splitting them into wood. The Colonel thought to replenish our finances with the beginning of a barrel stave company. The woods around us had unlimited supplies of trees, free and there for the man who would work to bring them in. With the boys help, we could sell enough staves to refill our empty pockets.

There was never a man and his sons who worked harder than the Colonel and his boys. With a good supply of staves, the boats were loaded. The Colonel and his two hired hands set out for New Orleans where the staves were to be sold.

The Colonel, not knowing much about boats, learned the hardest way possible that his hired help didn't know much either. When they tried to tie the boats up for the night, one of the boats got away and went on down the river without them. With the men in the other boat they set out after the first one, hoping to catch and recover the runaway boat. The river was rough and they came upon a backup of fallen trees and limbs; they plowed right into them knocking a hole in the boat. As the boat was sinking the two men jumped into the water leaving the Colonel inside the boat. As the boat was filling with water, the Colonel had to take an ax and try to get out. He was only half way out when he became stuck in the hole. He managed to get the attention of the men who then pulled him out through the hole tearing his clothes off in the process. He had almost lost his life again.

Author's Note:
This incident got David out of the stave making business and he was broke again. But with an undefeated spirit, he was soon back into the swing of life's ups and downs.

Antique Fabrics Gallery

Congressman David Crockett, served for three terms.
Image courtesy of Tennessee State Library and Archives

1827 – The Colonel becomes a Congressman

After the loss of the boats and staves, The Colonel returned home. There was talk around the country for him to run for Congress again. Colonel Alexander had beat The Colonel the last time around, by convincing everyone it was due to him and his tariff that the price of cotton had gone up. Cotton was now down, even with the tariffs.

At the Colonel's request, I made him a big old buckskin shirt with a large pocket on each side. In one he carried a twist of tobacco, in the other a skin of liquor. Whenever he met up with a voter, he offered him a dram of liquor. In order to drink the dram, the man would spit out his quid. The Colonel would visit with the voter awhile, telling his funny stories and by the time the fellow had finished his drink, The Colonel had made a fast friend. When the drink was finished, The Colonel took out the twist and gave the man another chew.

During one of The Colonel's speeches a flock of guinea hens interrupted him. Everyone started to laugh. The Colonel noted to the crowd that even the guineas were calling, "Crockett, Crockett, Crockett." Guinea hens are the noisiest of little critters and make very good watch-outs for strangers. At the smallest disturbance, guineas will run around making crack-et sounds until someone shoos them out of hearing distance. I too loved the sound of guineas as one could tell by their sound, if there was something to worry on or if all was just right.

The many folksy remarks of The Colonel brought laughter, and made him very popular with the voters. He won the seat for Congress by twenty-seven hundred and forty-eight votes.

Author's Note:
It is a Politicians' stock-in-trade to blame the opposing party for all the ills while taking credit for anything happening that will make the people more prosperous. Cotton was a large part of the economy of the South. Ups and downs could make or break even small planters.

Antique Fabrics Gallery

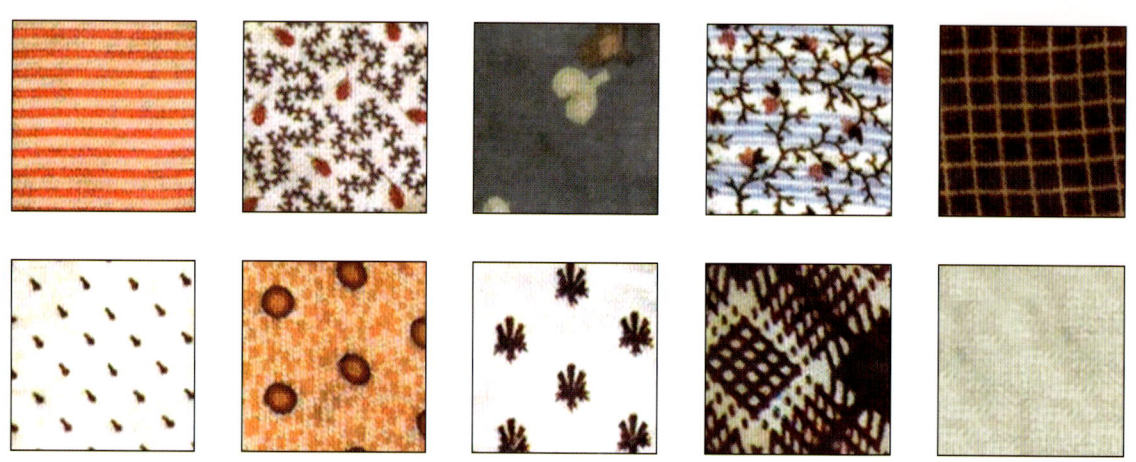

The Old farmstead - Going back to a place that was once a place of joy and great sadness brings back memories too terrible to think about, and then it is gone forever. Image courtesy Swannanoa Museum, Swannanoa, North Carolina

1829 – *A great time of sadness*

Our sadness began early in January when my niece Rebecca, daughter of my sister Mary Burgin, was staying with us and playing outside with the other children. The children were all running around happily playing their games, when the tragedy struck.

We had a walking mill grinding some sugar cane. Oxen tied to a brace turned the grinders, extracting the juice which ran into a long trough where the juice was cooked and made into molasses. Little Rebecca while taking a break from her running stopped by one of the outside posts. When the brace came around she was caught between the post and brace, killing her instantly. Our two daughters, Margaret Crockett and Margaret Patton, who were now young women, wept something terrible over the loss of their little cousin.

Just a short time later, we received word that my mother, Rebecca, was very ill. I packed my horse, and along with other family members started the trek to North Carolina, all the time hoping that she would still be with us when we arrived. We were fortunate to spend some time with our mother. She is buried in the little cemetery next to where the old Patton Meeting House had stood. The Meeting House had long since burned down, taking all its wonderful memories with it.

While we were still in Swannanoa, we learned that Uncle Elijah Patton, the father of my first husband James, had also passed on. There is an old saying that death comes to a family in threes. I prayed that we would have no more deaths in our family for a good long time to come.

Before returning to the Obion, I learned that the two hundred-fifty acre farmstead, built by James and myself, now belonged to The Colonel, as my present husband, and to my children, George and Margaret Patton, who was now married to Hance Campbell McWhorter.

Author's Note:
Elijah had taken a fifty year lease on Cove Spring Creek, where David and Elizabeth were married. Married women could not own property so her half-share went to her husband, David Crockett. By filing a suit, David was able to break the lease as the lessee had since died. Sources: Legal Documents and Letter from David Crockett to George Patton of Swannanoa, North Carolina January 27, 1829.

Antique Fabrics Gallery

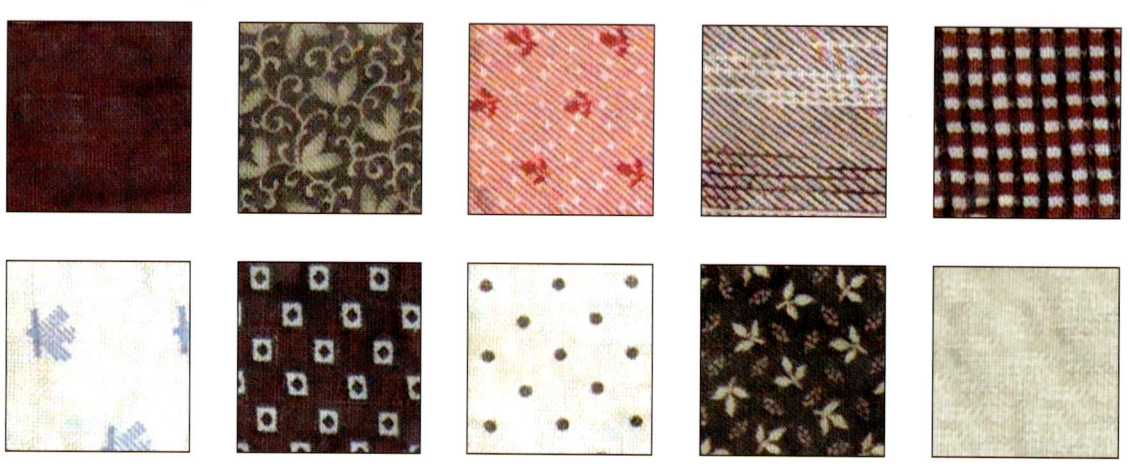

Bed in the living area of the Old Crockett Cabin in Rutherford, Gibson County, Tennessee. Photo by Helen Widener

1830 Spring - Home to Obion

My sisters and I stayed on with Papa until the spring. I wanted Papa to come home with me. My brother, George, had long since taken over the running of all things in North Carolina. As Papa was nearing ninety years of age, I wanted him with me. My sisters wanted him with them also. Papa talked to us all and invited all my sisters and their husbands to move with him and me to the Obion River. He promised to buy land for each of them as a good start.

I had sorely missed Papa, living so far away. He was still a hardy man, but like us all, age would soon begin to rule his life. My sisters and their husbands were eager to take Papa up on his offer and move to Gibson County, Tennessee. Since The Colonel was also a Tennessee Congressman, there was no lack of lively life. There were always frolics happening wherever my husband might be. Also, with all my sisters around us we could have quilting frolics and visit the day away while the children played.

Upon reaching the Obion and home, Papa quickly found and bought a Thousand acres of land shared between my sisters and their husbands. We were all so happy to be together again as we were a very close and loving family. The teachings of Momma and Papa were to love and care for each other. Each of our gatherings were met with much hugging, kissing and laughter, as we caught up on the everyday happenings of our life. We quilted together, shared recipes and foods from the garden. We all had the same plants and trees around our house, because what one had the others shared. We were family.

Author's Note:
The last comes from my personal knowledge of the Patton Family through descendants of George Patton. They showed much affection for each other and the sharing of meals together. It was a great privilege for me to know and love descendant Samuel Isaac Patton, known as Papaw.

Antique Fabrics Gallery

Crockett Fire Place and cooking pots, Crockett Cabin, Rutherford, Gibson County, Tennessee. Photo by Helen Widener

1830 - Another defeat for The Colonel

In the Congress, there was a terrible split between the thinking of The Colonel and his former General, Andrew Jackson, now the President of the United States. Being against Jackson was unpardonable in our area. Few knew of Jackson's deeds. He had fought sixteen duels, killing fourteen men. I didn't hold much with the so-called "honor" of a duel. I also remembered the Creek War, when Jackson had shot one of the soldiers, not yet a full-grown man. The soldier had served the time he had signed up to do and he desperately needed to go home to care for his family during the winter months. Other men had also served their time and were planning to go home to care for their families. Jackson pulled out his pistol and shot the young man where he stood. The volunteer service they had signed up for had become one of enforced service.

Jackson's men played dirty tricks by setting up speeches for The Colonel during the election; since he knew not of the speeches he could not be present to give one. Jackson's men then used the opportunity, in of the absence of The Colonel, to smear his good name, causing him to lose the election. It was hard to believe The Colonel had ever backed General Jackson for President of our great Country.

The next two years were a pleasure for me to have my husband home. He spent much of his time at the hunt always bringing in game. We received the best of meats and skins of any family in the country as well as plenty left over for sale to those who had not the skills or need to provide for themselves.

Author's Note:
The families of both David and Elizabeth were growing up and beginning to marry and have families of their own. It must have been very satisfying to have raised the eight children between them to adulthood.

Antique Fabrics Gallery

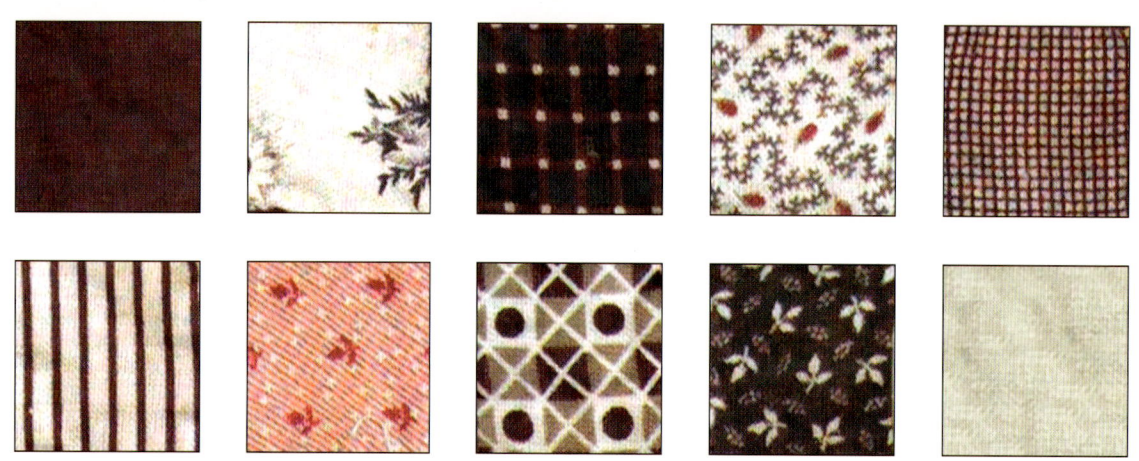

Wooden churn like those used by frontier women during the time that Elizabeth lived. Virginia Cultural Museum, Staunton Virginia. Photo by Helen Widener

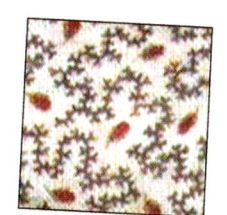

1832 - Down but not out

Two years had passed since The Colonel's defeat for Congress. He was now more than ready to take on "The Liberals" in another run for office.

Districts which were once under The Colonel's jurisdiction had been redrawn or gerrymandered to cut out most of the people who had voted for him before.

The Colonel had now broken completely with the Jackson Legislature. Many of Jackson's friends and colleges became immensely wealthy on lands purchased at a small price from the Indians. The Colonel was very vocal on the disbursement of the lands and the removal of the Indians. Having acquired the lands, The Colonel wanted to pass a Bill that would allow people who had homesteaded an opportunity to buy the land. This was in direct opposition to Jackson who was himself becoming very wealthy on the broken promises to the Indians.

After all the intrigues, the people themselves found they didn't like being transferred around like hogs, horses and cattle in the market. A hard fought battle had The Colonel ahead by two hundred and two votes.

The world of my family, outside the doings of The Colonel, went ahead as it has always gone. I milked the cows, churned the milk and made the butter. There was never a lack of either on our table. There was always a buckskin outfit in the mending basket and a new one in the works. If there was a thorn thicket anywhere around, The Colonel was sure to go straight through after a bear, rather than lose an opportunity to bring home more game even when our larder was full. For sure, there was always a neighbor who needed meat for his table even if we didn't.

Author's Note:
There were numerous incidents in the Autobiography of David Crockett where he provides or shares the animals he killed with families less fortunate than himself. He was most generous in giving away meat

55

Antique Fabrics Gallery

Version of North Carolina Lilly Quilt made in 1849 – owned by Nina Hall of Coppell, Texas. Photo by Helen Widener

1832 – Death of Robert Patton

    With the death of Papa my world as I had always known it, came to an end. I had never given much thought about the importance of Papa in my life, his world of wisdom and the tender teachings and love of a father. To me he was just Papa, always there in a time of need. I had realized of late that he was not always the way that I remembered him from my youth. At the age of ninety he had become an old man. Still, he seemed to be a man of some remaining vigor and did much of the work on his place himself.

    We buried Papa on a bluff overlooking the Obion River, each of us bringing along a river stone to lay upon his cairn, as was done in Scotland. Papa loved the river and had, since his arrival in America, lived near one. It was fitting to bury him in a place he loved.

    Papa had always been a good provider and had amassed a good amount of wealth. It was with great dismay that I learned he had not given to his children equally. Papa had blessed The Colonel and me with great gifts of property, far more than my sisters. Through a miscalculation of acres, my sister, Catherine had received more land from Papa than my other sisters but not enough to justify Papa's leaving her only $10.00. As is often the case with the death of a parent, the loving family becomes one estranged from each other, losing family ties that have always bound them together. It was most difficult for me, as The Colonel was one of the executors as well as a benefactor.

Author's Note:
Two of the sisters received only ten dollars each as they had supposedly already received their shares. Catherine Ann McWhorter was one of the slighted sisters, which made it especially difficult for Elizabeth. George and Margaret Patton, Elizabeth's children, were both married to their cousins who were Catherine's children. Lawsuits followed.

Antique Fabrics Gallery

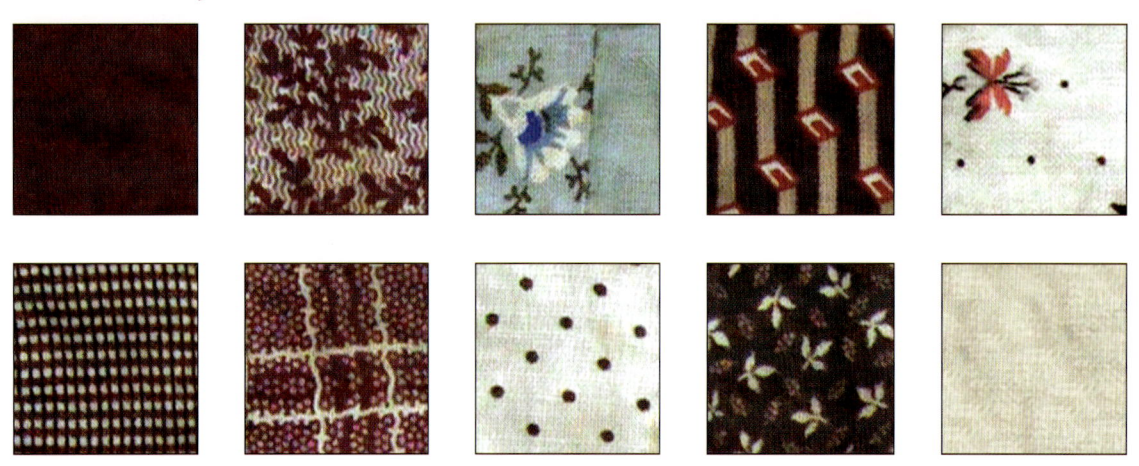

An older David Crockett in hunting suit probably painted during his last term of office before he left for Texas and the Alamo. Courtesy of Tennessee State Archives and Library. The Crockett image on the back of this book was digitally removed and enhanced from this painting.

1833-1835 - The last of Congress

The Franklin County property of my first husband was sold for twelve hundred dollars. My son George had married Rhoda McWhorter and now had their first child, James Calvin Patton. With the money he had received for his share of the sale, he purchased our farmstead and twenty-five acres from The Colonel, who was in a desperate financial way after the expenses of running a campaign.

The Colonel took a lease on a cabin where we lived for a time. The Colonel stayed in congress for two more terms. His final defeat for congress was in the fall of 1835. He had taken an extensive trip up north. Many people were declaring that he should run for President and he had in mind to run, as a Whig, he had many changes in mind for the greedy members of congress that were ruining the country. Unbelievably, he lost his bid for congress, effectively destroying his chances of becoming President of the United States.

The Colonel, after 14 years, had had a surfeit of politics and just couldn't digest anymore. For now, he said, "They might all go to hell, and he would go to Texas."

I believe he didn't mind the loss of the election. Texas was calling his name, and he had already determined to go there long before the election was over. We had been hearing reports of the wonders of Texas for some time, as many Americans were moving there. The Mexican Government had promised four thousand acres of land to men who would bring their families and settle in Texas. Mexico needed people to fight the Indians for the land.

Author's Note:
During this time, David and Elizabeth moved two more times and lived in different counties. The last cabin, where David and Elizabeth lived is located in Rutherford, Gibson County, Tennessee. Matilda, 15 years old at the time of her father's death, was still living at home with Elizabeth.

Antique Fabrics Gallery

The Battle of the Alamo began February 23rd and ended with the fall of The Alamo on March 6, 1836 in San Antonio, Texas.
Image courtesy of New York Public Library

FALL OF THE ALAMO.

1835 – 1836 - *The Fall of The Alamo*

The Colonel came in from hunting one evening and said, "Well Bet, I am beat and I'm off for Texas." He planned for us all to start as early as possible at the beginning of the New Year. It was a great shock to me, as I didn't want to leave my family and start a new life in another country. I didn't have good feelings about this move and persuaded him to let me and the children remain until he had everything set up. He could return to get us.

After he had put his affairs in order, given a big barn dance the likes of which had not been seen in our county before, he was ready to start for Texas. The morning they set out, The Colonel was wearing a new hunting suit and his favorite coon-skin cap. He was still a fine looking figure of a man and I would sorely miss the constant activity his presence inspired. Two of my brothers-in-law were going with The Colonel, as well as my nephew, William Patton. Four thousand acres of land, free for the settling, was a great inducement to many men.

It was a very short few weeks of time when my brothers-in-law returned and told us of Texas' Declaration of Independence from Mexico. There would be fighting. The Colonel and William were on their way to a place called "The Alamo." A month later we received more news that The Alamo was under siege with one hundred eighty-nine men inside. Only days later we received the terrible news that The Alamo had fallen and all the men were dead, including The Colonel. I was once again the widow of a fighting man. My nephew, William Patton, was spared the fate of his uncle, because he had been sent to General Sam Houston, with a message, requesting additional soldiers for the Alamo.

Author's Note:
The Alamo's fall resounded throughout the southern states and a vast army marched into Texas with these words on their lips, "Remember The Alamo." After 172 years, The Alamo stands proud in San Antonio, Texas, under the care of The Daughters of The Republic of Texas.

61

Antique Fabrics Gallery

The inside of the trunk is completely covered with newspaper and includes a fabricated story from The New York Cortland Advocate, dated May 12, 1836. The Stagecoach trunk is from the collection of Nina Hall.
Photo by Helen Widener

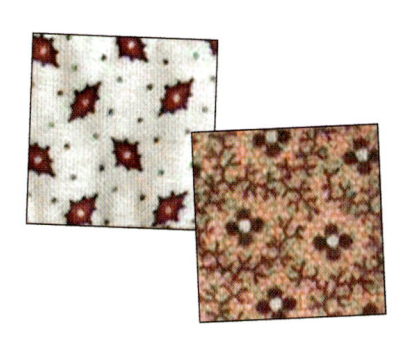

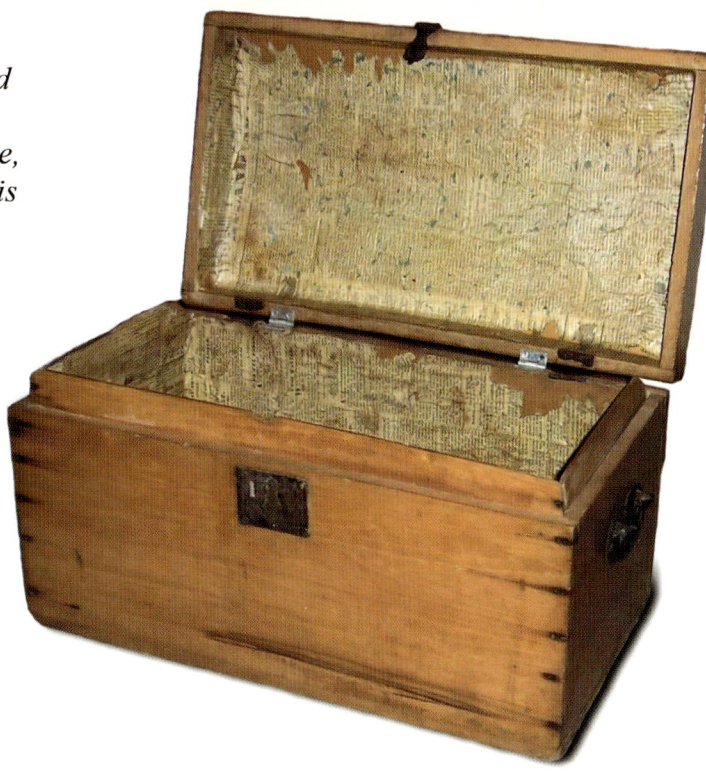

1836-Too many rumors

The stories we heard were too many and too horrible. All our family was greatly distressed by the death of The Colonel and what we heard. One of the early stories was that when the Mexicans had taken over The Alamo, The Colonel and some of the other men were still alive. Santa Anna, Mexico's General, ordered the men killed. The Mexicans instantly fell on our men brutally mutilating them with bayonets. In the same instant, The Colonel leaped like a panther at Santa Anna and died with the thrust of a dozen bayonets.

Another rumor, the cruelest of them all, published by a newspaper called The Cortland Advocate in New York, had The Colonel sorely wounded but still alive and recovering from his wounds in the home of friends near San Antonio. It was a pure fiction, made up to sell newspapers. The owners of the paper cared nothing for the distress of the family which they had so cruelly given false hope.

The men of Tennessee, Arkansas and all other states, were so outraged they volunteered by the thousands to fight for the Independence of Texas. Across Texas they fought, winning some battles and losing others. The final battle for the Republic of Texas happened at San Jacinto. By retreat, General Houston had maneuvered the opposing army into an area where they could not escape. Santa Anna was with that part of the Mexican troops. The ensuing battle was a complete destruction of the Mexican forces. Santa Anna slipped away during the fighting, but was later found and captured. When he was brought before General Houston he was wearing a rounded coat and blue pantaloons, the clothing of a common soldier. Mexican prisoners gave away his identity by yelling out "El Presidente!"

Author's Note:
The fall of The Alamo happened on March 6, 1836. The Battle of San Jacinto lasted only 22 minutes, beginning and ending on April 21, 1836. Santa Anna was shown the mercy he had denied the men of The Alamo, and later served many terms as the President of Mexico.

63

Antique Fabrics Gallery

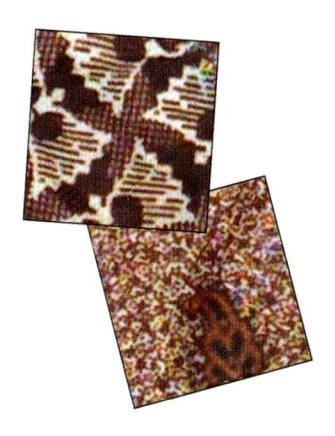

Crockett Cabin in Rutherford, Gibson County, Tennessee. The cabin was moved and rebuilt from parts of the original cabin and another cabin in the area. Photo by Helen Widener

1836-1850 - The Widow Crockett

After the death of The Colonel, only Matilda and I lived in our rented cabin. My lease would be effective until 1838. We would just scuffle along. I was out on my horse almost daily helping with the birthing of a baby or tending the sick. The families were always pressing me to take chickens and pork, legs of venison or fruits and vegetables. This is the only way people could express their thanks for my help. We were very poor, but the needs of our minds and bodies were well met.

A year after The Colonel's death, Matilda married Thomas Tyson, leaving me in the cabin alone. It was a lonesome time even with the frequent visits of my family. I still missed and mourned the death of my husband. When the cabin's lease expired, I went to live with my daughter, Matilda, and her family. My health was good, and I worked for my keep by birthing and helping with the children and household. I also brought in a little extra on the side with my healing.

The years passed along and I heard nothing on the land grants that families of the men who fought for the Republic of Texas were suppose to receive. In 1849, Matilda's husband died leaving her with two boys and two girls, the oldest only twelve.

In 1852, the long awaited news came that the heirs of Colonel David Crockett would receive a league of land. It sounded like so much land! In addition to the land, we received a certificate for The Colonel's service to The Alamo for twenty-four dollars ($24.00). My children had already determined that we would claim the land when it was available.

Author's Note:
There is nothing written about how Elizabeth managed to survive after David's death. There was little property and goods remaining in David's estate. Accounts of grandchildren say she often cared for the sick. The 1850 Tennessee census has Elizabeth living with the widowed Matilda

Antique Fabrics Gallery

In the early 1850s immigrants began to arrive in droves as the land had become available to those men who had fought for the Republic of Texas. Immigrants Camp Image courtesy of the New York Public Library

1854 – GTT "Gone To Texas"

It was to be a new beginning for me and for my children. Those who had decided to accompany me to Texas were my sons, George Patton, Robert Crockett and daughter Rebecca Halford. There were also a number of other relatives and friends who would join our wagon train. It was two years before we could get everything settled. The children going with me purchased the shares of Texas property belonging to John Wesley Crockett, William Crockett now deceased, Margaret Flowers and my daughter, Matilda Wilson. My half interest in the property, I deeded to my children, George Patton, Margaret McWhorter, Robert Crockett, Rebecca Halford and Matilda Wilson.

We started out in covered wagons drawn by oxen. There were many rivers that had to be crossed and hills to climb. Rains caused muddy trails almost impossible to use. After a time on the trail we became used to the hardships and settled into a daily routine. We headed for a small town in Texas called Waxahachie. Upon arriving, we set up camp outside of town. We first hired an attorney to represent us in the acquisition of the property. We then hired a surveyor to locate the land and mark it off. The final amount of our land was three hundred and twenty acres located on Rutgers Creek in Johnson County. The rest of the land was used as payment to the Surveyor and the Attorney for their services.

It was a hard tough trail that we followed out to the property on Rutgers Creek. We lived out of our wagons until the men could put up some cabins for the families. We all helped each other, for that was the only way to survive in the wilderness of the country. Though we had little trouble with the Indians, we were always aware of their presence.

Author's Note:
The area of Rutgers Creek is now located in Acton, Hood (formerly Johnson) County, Texas. The League of Crockett Land covered areas on both sides of the Brazos River. Elizabeth deeded her share of the Texas land to her children. They also bought the shares of land from the children of David Crockett.

Antique Fabrics Gallery

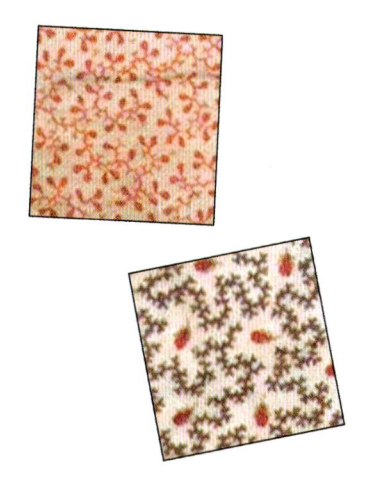

The whole state of Texas has been blessed with beautiful sunrises and sunsets. In 2008 the author took this photo of a Texas morning-sky.

1854-1860 - Texas Sunrise and death of Elizabeth

Texas was a hard land. The amount of work that went into the tilling of the land and the building of our cabins was more than I could ever have imagined. The grounds were broken and crops planted only to be nearly burned to death by the hot Texas sun before they could be harvested. The Colonel had cast his lot with Texas and so had we. It was make a go or die in the trying.

Times were very hard, and I had gone to care for some orphaned children. Mr. Dyer, a friend and neighbor, thought he should write a letter to the State of Texas for assistance as we were in such desperate circumstances. I told him to go ahead if he thought it was the right thing to do. The state looked into our circumstances and conceded that we, indeed, were very poor. However, they had no laws for the assistance of widows and children. They denied any claim for help to us, as they did not want others to also ask for assistance

Severe hardships and age began to take its toll on me. And I often stayed for a time with each of my children who lived near me.

Author's Note:
It was the habit of Elizabeth to take a morning walk. It was one of those chilly beautiful Texas winter mornings when Elizabeth left for her usual walk. A Texan can imagine the morning sky splashed with colors of orange, yellows and lavender. Elizabeth paused by the gate on her return. She then proceeded to the cabin. As she was coming to the front door she wavered and family members rushed to catch her as she fell. She was carried to the bed where she died later in the evening, January 31, 1860. Pierce Ward, a young orphan, who had lived with the Crockett family and later became a Senator, presented a Bill to the Texas Legislature at Austin which requested $2,000.00 for a monument in Acton, Texas as a memorial to Elizabeth and other brave frontier women. The Monument is of a frontier woman, a hand shading her eyes forever scanning the horizon for a husband who never returns.

Dear Readers: My writing of Elizabeth's story has caused in me extreme ups and downs of emotions; from the sadness at her loss of both husbands, to anger at the injustices imposed on women of the time; then to the incredible feeling of wonder when the reproduction quilt was finished. Thank you all for being a part of Scraps of Life.

Helen Ogden Widener

Antique Fabrics Gallery

Sashes, Cornerstone and Additional Fabric Blocks

No. 6127 PUBLIC DEBT Second Class, "B."

OF THE

LATE REPUBLIC OF TEXAS.

This is to Certify, That David Crockett dec'd pr. heirs has, under the provisions of An Act of the Legislature of the State of Texas, entitled An Act to extend the provisions of "An Act to provide for ascertaining the Debt of the late Republic of Texas," approve February 7, 1853, filed with the Auditor and Comptroller, A claim for Services at the Alamo in 1836

amounting to Twenty four Dollars; which is sufficiently authenticated to authorize the auditing of the same under the laws of the late Republic of Texas. Said claim, according to the data before us, is worth Twenty four Dollars, in par funds, as having been at that rate so available to the Government.

In Testimony Whereof, We have hereunto set our hands and affixed our seals of office, at Austin, this 2nd day of December A. D. 1854

(A)

[signature], Comptroller.

[signature], Auditor.

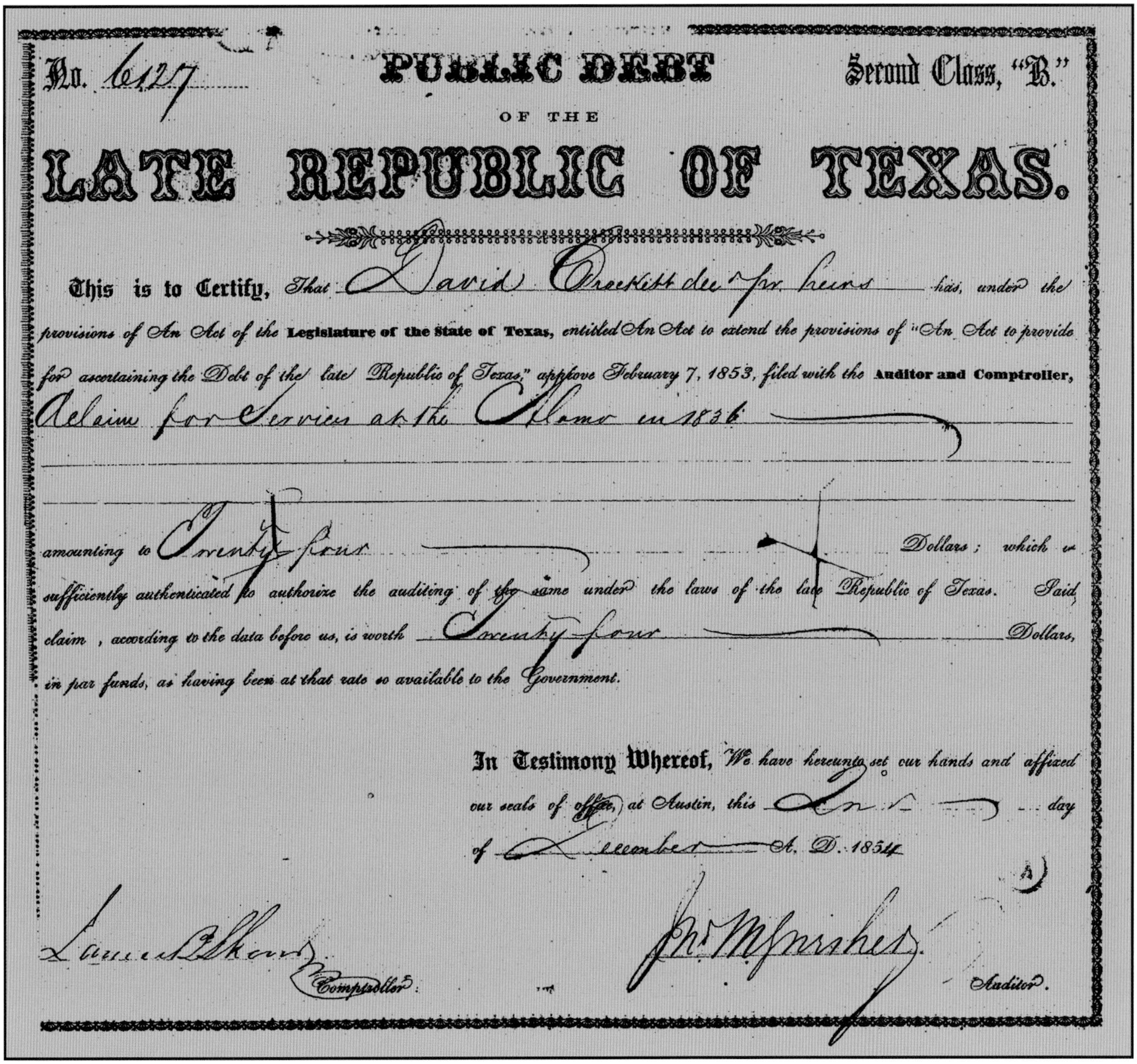

The above image is a photo copy of a Certificate issued by the State of Texas to the heirs of David Crockett for his service at The Alamo and the late Republic of Texas.

Dallas Herald.

FEBRUARY 29, 1860.

DALLAS, DALLAS COUNTY, TEXAS.

Mrs. Elizabeth Crockett

Last week we chronicled the death of this venerable and most estimable lady. A friend has sent as us the following particulars, connected with her eventful life.

Mrs. Elizabeth Crockett, relict of the Hon. Davy Crockett, died in the 74th year of her age. She was born in Buncombe county, N. C., in May, 1788. Her maiden name was Patton. She was married to James Patton, her cousin, and removed with him to Franklin county, Tenn. He was killed fighting for his country, in the celebrated Creek War. By him she had two children. Subsequently she was married to the lamented Crockett, who fel at the Alamo; thus she lost her second husband as her first, in battle. By her second husband she had three children---one son and two daughters. Robert P. Crockett, her son, now lives in Johnson county. Rebecca Elvira, her eldest daughter, consort of Rev. Mr. Halford, lives also in Johnson county; and Matilda, the youngest, lives in Tennessee.

In 1855 she removed from Tennessee to Texas, and settled on lands, the gift of a grateful State to the widow and heirs of Davy Crockett, her heroic defender. It is a matter of just pride to every citizen of Texas that the widow of Davy Crockett found a home in her old age, and after her three score years and ten were fulfilled, a grave on the soil consecrated by his blood--the gift of the country of his adoption. The grave of his widow and the home of his children will make Johnson county a place of pilgrimage to many.

Mrs. Crockett was a member of the Methodist Episcopal Church, South, and died in the full triumph of her holy faith. That she was a woman of many and rare virtues, the writer and many others in Johnson county, her neighbors, can bear witness.

A NEIGHBOR AND FRIEND OF THE DECEASED.

A copy of Elizabeth's obituary taken from microfilm library, Texas History Department at the Dallas Public Library, Dallas, Texas.

Elizabeth Crockett's memorial statue erected 1913 at her burial sight. Acton, Hood County, Texas (Photo by Helen Widener)

SCRAPS of LIFE

Scraps of Life Quilt Instructions

The original quilt made by Elizabeth Patton Crockett is made scraps of the families clothing. Some of the fabrics appear only one or two times in the entire quilt while others repeat frequently. The wealth of reproduction fabrics available on the quilting market give many possibilities when creating this quilt. Refer back to the photos of individual blocks when choosing your fabrics. Select fabrics that match as closely as possible to the original fabrics, or select fabrics to coordinate from your own stash of fabrics. To preserve the look of the original quilt, match color value and contrast in the blocks, while using reproduction fabric available.

The original quilt is pieced from individual 1.50 inch squares of fabric; however, these instructions make use of modern rotary cutting and strip piecing methods. The ***quilt is challenging*** and the instructions written are for an experienced quilter. It is assumed that persons undertaking a reproduction of this quilt are familiar with using a rotary cutter system, strip piecing and good pressing techniques. All blocks are to be pieced using exactly the same techniques, only the fabric choices differ from block to block. The instructions for a block are presented only one time, and are used for each block. There are 30 pieced quilt blocks, approximately 12 x 12 inches square for a 5 x 6 block layout. Finished size is approximately 72 x 86 inches.

Fabric requirements (all fabrics 100% cotton):
1 fat quarter for block centers (or use a variety of scraps)
518 strips 1.50 x 22 inches. These can be cut from a variety of fat quarters or from yardage. You can get 37 fat quarters or about 9.25 yards of fabric. This is a scrappy quilt though, so the more fabrics the scrappier the quilt will look.
1.75 yards white or cream muslin for the outside row of squares
2.50 yards sashing fabric
.75 yards setting stones fabric
6 yards for backing (seamed vertically)
.50 yard for 2" French fold binding (cut on the straight grain of fabric)

Required Tools:
Sewing machine with .25" presser foot or seam guide
Rotary Cutter and large mat
Rotary Ruler 18"x 6" or 12.5" square (since most of the cuts are 1.5" it is easier to work with a ruler that has a built in half inch on one side)
Neutral thread for piecing
Pins (glass head straight pins size 26 extra fine work well)
Iron and ironing board
Seam ripper

Tools that may come in handy: Portable pressing board to lay out strips as the block sewn together, fabric glue or tape for adhering swatches to sample sheets, Plastic zip bags for holding leftover scraps or strips

Fabric Swatch Card (copy this page to make a swatch card for each block)

Fabric 1 (center)

Fabric 2

Fabric 3

Fabric 4

Fabric 5

Fabric 6

Fabric 7

Fabric 8

Fabric 9

Fabric 10 (white or neutral)

Cutting Instructions

NOTE: Fabric 1 is best cut into 1.5" squares as only one is used in each block. Cut 30 squares 1.5" and set aside. It is also helpful to cut 60 squares of fabric 1.5" of fabric number10 to use in block construction.

For each Block:

Cut 1 strip 1.5" x 22" from Fabrics 2 and 3

Cut 2 strips 1.5" x 22" from Fabrics 4, 5 and 6

Cut 3 strips 1.5" x 22" from Fabrics 7, 8, 9 and 10

Piecing Instructions

Before sewing sets, cut a small piece of each one of the fabrics from the strip and affix to the swatch card in order. Refer to the card when sewing the strips sets and when piecing the block.

Strip set 1: Sew strips 2 – 10 together in that order. Press the seam allowances towards strip 2.

Strip set 2: Sew strips 4-10 together in that order. Press the seam allowances towards strip 4

Strip set 3: Sew strips 7 – 10 together in that order. Press the seam allowances towards strip 7.

Cut each set into 1.5" strips, making sure to cut 12 from each strip set.

Row Instructions:

The block is assembled in rows diagonally. Row 1 is the Center Row, and they are numbered moving out from the center.

Row 1 (make 1):

Using 2 pieces from strip set 1 and one center square, assemble row 1 and press all seams TOWARDS the center

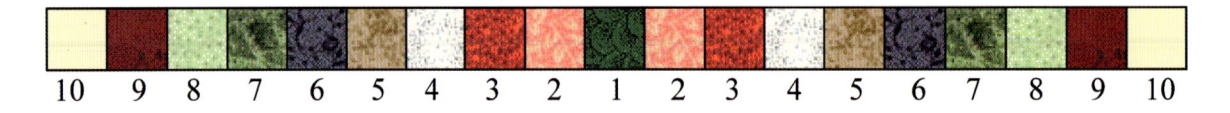

10 9 8 7 6 5 4 3 2 1 2 3 4 5 6 7 8 9 10

Row 2 (make 2):

Using 2 pieces of strip set 1, remove fabric 2 from one of the pieces and seam them together. Press all seams AWAY from the center.

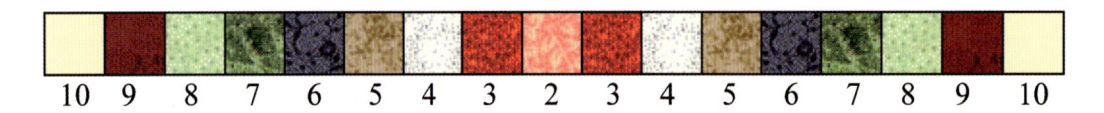

10 9 8 7 6 5 4 3 2 3 4 5 6 7 8 9 10

Row 3 (make 2):

Using 2 pieces from strip set 1, remove fabric 2 from one piece and fabrics 2 and 3 from the second piece and seam them together. Press all seams TOWARDS the center

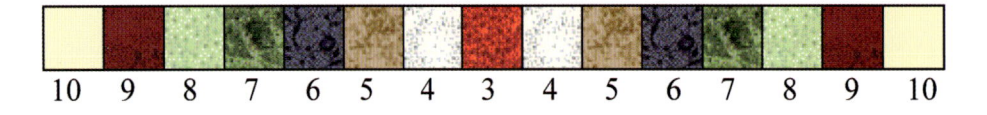

10 9 8 7 6 5 4 3 4 5 6 7 8 9 10

Row 4 (make 2):

Using 1 piece from strip set 1, remove fabrics 2, 3 and 4. Seam to a piece from strip set 2. Press all seams AWAY from the center.

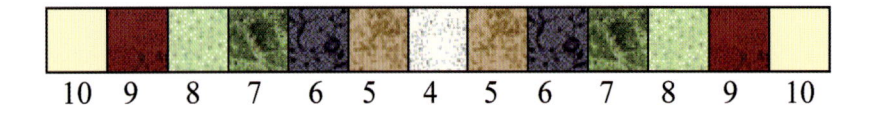

10 9 8 7 6 5 4 5 6 7 8 9 10

Row 5 (make 2):

Using 2 pieces from strip set 2, remove fabric 4 from one piece and fabrics 4 and 5 from the second piece and seam together. Press all seams TOWARDS the center.

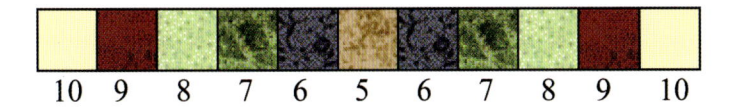

10 9 8 7 6 5 6 7 8 9 10

Row 6 (make 2):

Using 2 pieces from strip set 2 remove fabrics 4 and 5 from one piece and fabrics 4, 5 and 6 from the second piece and seam them together. Press all seams AWAY from the center.

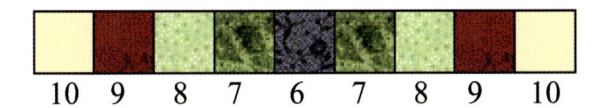

10 9 8 7 6 7 8 9 10

Row 7 (make 2):

Using 1 piece from strip set 2 remove fabrics 4, 5, 6 and 7 and seam to one piece from strip set 3. Press all seams TOWARDS the center.

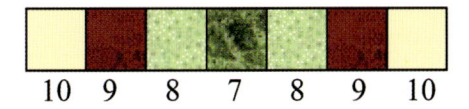

10 9 8 7 8 9 10

Row 8 (make 2):

Using 2 pieces from strip set 3 remove fabric 7 from one piece, and fabrics 7 and 8 from the other piece and seam them together. Press all seams AWAY from the center.

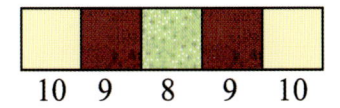

10 9 8 9 10

Row 9 (make 2):

Using 2 pieces from strip set 3 remove fabrics 7 and 8 from one piece and fabrics 7, 8 and 9 from the other piece and seam them together. Press all seams TOWARDS the center.

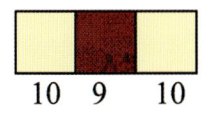

10 9 10

Row 10:
Use two squares of white or natural fabric number 10 previously cut.

Block Instructions:

Lay out the strips in order and sew them together starting from the center. Because of the pressing instructions, the seam allowances should nest as the rows are assembled. Use the following diagram, which shows half the block from the center out. It can be useful to lay out all the strips on the portable pressing board and work from that rather than working from piles. When sewing strips together always start sewing on the longer strip into the shorter strip so that the end of the shorter strip is included in the seam.

Row 10

Row 9

Row 8

Row 7

Row 6

Row 5

Row 4

Row 3

Row 2

Row 1

When the block is complete press the strips AWAY from strip set 1 and make sure the block is square. **DO NOT TRIM THE POINTS OFF OF THE FABRIC NUMBER 10 SQUARES AT THIS TIME!!** The blocks will be trimmed after the sashing is attached to help manage the bias edges.

Using these instructions, and the color/fabric chart for each block, complete all 30 blocks.

Sashing and corner stones:

When looking at the untrimmed block, the 'inside' point of the V between the fabric number 10 squares is the unfinished edge of the block. This point is where the unfinished edge of a fabric number 10 square meets the adjacent fabric 10 square, and should be approximately .25" out from the point of fabric 9. Note where the arrows are located in the picture:

Measure all 30 blocks across the middle from the inside point to inside point. Take an average of this measurement. The blocks should be 12.5" unfinished, but everyone sews differently and the quilt will lay flatter if the sashing is cut to fit the existing blocks.

Cut 45 squares 2.5" x 2.5" for the setting stone fabric.

Cut 71 strips 2.5" x the average block measurement of the fabric used for the sashing strips.

It is easiest to work across in rows. Attach the sashing strips and blocks together in horizontal rows. Make 6 rows with 5 blocks in each row. (Note: the block has been simplified for the diagram). As each sashing strip is added, trim the extra points of fabric number 10 so that the seam line is an even .25 inch.

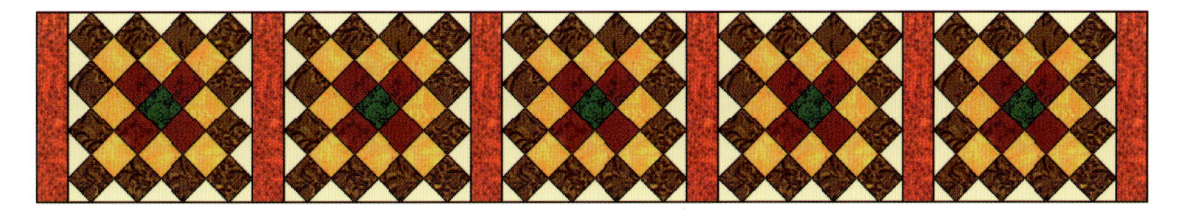

Using the remaining sashing strips and setting stones, piece together 6 rows starting and ending with a setting stone.

Assemble the rows into the finished quilt layout. Quilt and bind as desired.

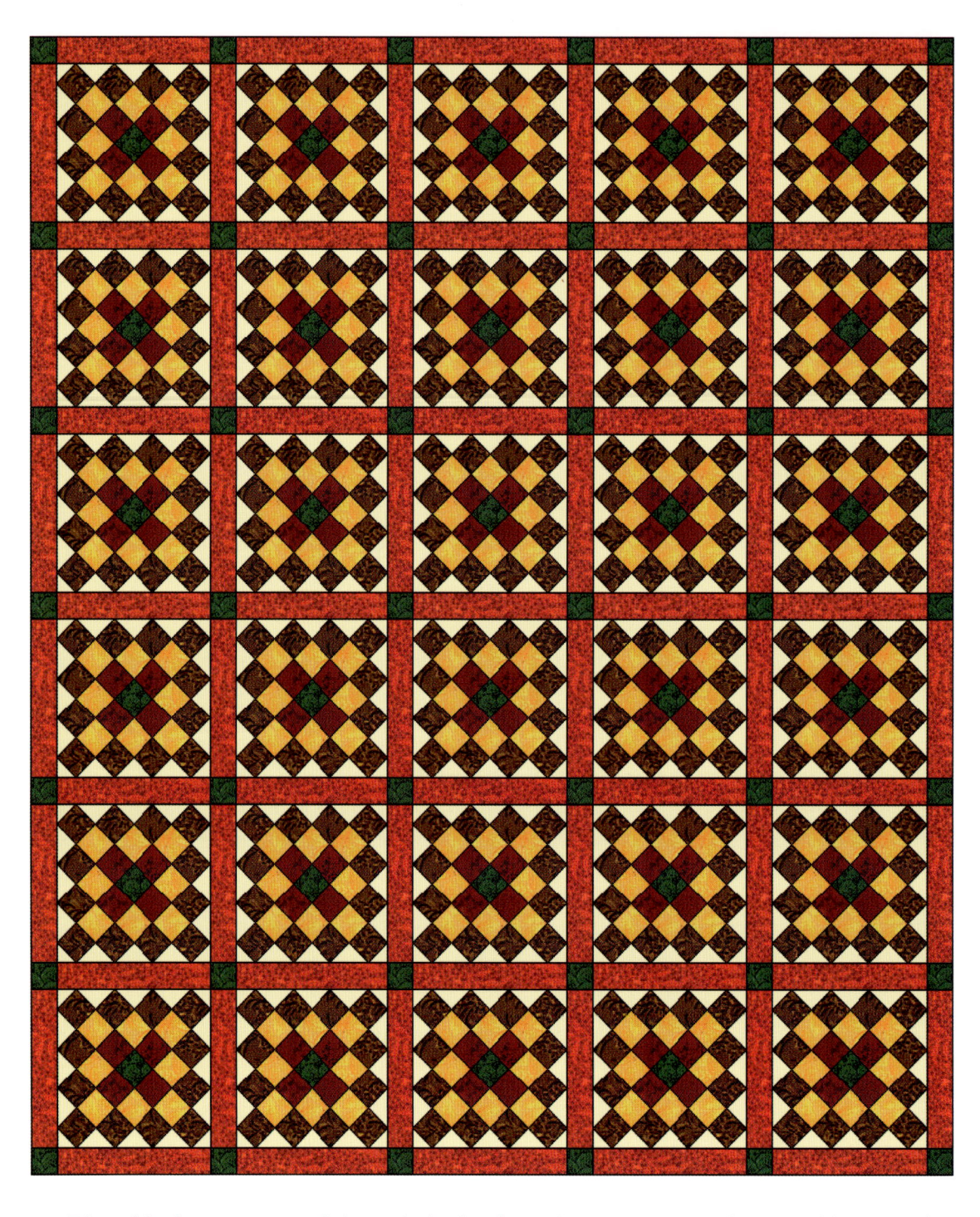

Place blocks as presented through the book or choose your own layout with rows of 5 blocks across and 6 blocks down

SCRAPS of LIFE

Acknowledgements
Genealogy and
Family Images

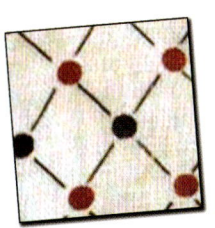

Acknowledgements

A special THANK YOU to all the wonderful people who have helped in putting this book together and there were so many.

Thanks to Bobbie Thomas for her editing and guidance. Thanks to Ben Thomas for the loan of the States Quilt made by his mother, Mrs. H.E. Thomas. Thanks to my husband, James Widener for pre-editing and encouragement. Thank you to my wonderful traveling and research companion, Ruth Lowery. Thanks to my son, Tad Browning for all the graphics work and photography. Thanks to Martha Wolf for writing the instructions for Scraps of Live. Thanks to the Meadowbrook Baptist Church Quilting Ladies, Nancy Norris, Ann Shafer, Cathy Goodwin and Joy Deaton for their help with the quilting. Thanks to Pam Pape-owner Magnolia Quiltworks for help in selecting the 19th Century Reproduction Fabrics used for the reproduction of Elizabeth's Quilt Top and Lone Star Quilts for fabric. Thanks to Jody Rhea for her friendship at my first meeting with the Irving Quilt Guild.

Thanks to all the others who have helped with guidance and Historical Information and photos. Ray Oden-Editor of Go Ahead, the Crockett Family Newsletter, Joe Bone and wife Sue-Curator of the Crockett Cabin in Rutherford, Tennessee, the last cabin where David and Elizabeth Crockett lived, Joy and Bobby Bland for Crockett photos, Regina Storms-Marcus Brothers Fabrics for her rescue when I ran out of a certain fabric, Nancy Jewell, Sharon and Amy Johnson, Aunt Ruth (Mrs. Robert Patton), Bobby, Donn, Cathey, Christine, Tina, Glenn, Mary Ann, Sandi and the late Jerry Murphy, all descendants of George Patton, and Graig Patton for Patton Family information. Ken Hendricks, descendant of Robert P. Crockett. Thanks to Janet Henderson-Antique Quilt Historian and Mayor, Joseph Roberson of the town of Ohatchee, Alabama. Thanks for sharing historical information to Gert Petterson and Virtus Edmundson.

Thanks to Nina Hall for the use of her quilt and coach trunk. Thanks to Rebecca Power, Isabel Gravel, Larry and Sherry Dunklin and Larry's mother, Madelene Dunklin's, for use of their quilts. Thanks to Georgia Matthews for her quilting knowledge and her work on the next reproduction quilt.

Thanks to all the Libraries, Museums and Archives that have helped with photos and historical information: Old Buncombe County Genealogical Society-Sandy Samz and William Trantham-Ashville North Carolina, Jill Jones-Swannanoa Valley Museum, Swannanoa, North Carolina. Gale Benfield-Burke County, North Carolina Public Library, Virginia Ellington- Librarian Franklin County Historical Society Winchester, Tennessee, Lanita Van Dyke Rutherford, Gibson County Tennessee, Mayor's office, Emily Walker-Gibson County Archives, Gibson County, Tennessee Memorial Library, Connie Bates-Gibson County Tennessee County Courthouse, Jay Richiuso-Tennessee State Library and Archives, Bill Simmons and John Anderson-Texas State Library and Archives Commission, Melba Hoover and Merle McNeece- Granbury Depot, Granbury Hood County, Texas, Samantha Smith-Asst. Librarian, Granbury Library, Dr. Bruce Winders-Historian and Curator of The Alamo, Witte Museum-San Antonio, Thomas Lisanti-New York Public Library for images, Mike Sutton Frontier Culture Museum Staunton, Virginia.

Helen Ogden Widener

Fabric Selections by - Owner
Pam Pape
Magnolia Quiltworks
pampape@sbcglobal.net

Martha Wolf
Quilting Instructor and
Dallas Quilting Show Volunteer
martha@pinwheelprodns.com
www.pinwheelprodns.com

Quilting Ladies of Meadowbrook Baptist Church - Irving, Texas
(left to right) Nancy Norris, Helen Widener, Ann Shafer
Cathy Goodwin and Joy Deaton

Patton Family Genealogy

Patton Family Genealogy: John Patton came to America ca.1755 and brought with him his sons, Robert, Elijah, Samuel and John Patton. The family first settled in Rowan County around the Old Fort in the Catawba River Valley. Robert received land grants for supplying wagons and wagon repairs to the *Over Mountain Men* on their way to the *Battle of Kings Mountain* the family probably moved into the Swannanoa Valley about 1882. At the time Swannanoa was still in Burke County. *(Note: History of Swannanoa.)*

Robert Patton Born: 1741/2 Ireland - Died: 11 November 1832, Gibson County, TN
Married: ca. 1780 **Rebecca Cathey** b. ca. 1766 Rowan County, N.C. Died: ca. 1828-29 Swannanoa, Buncombe Co., North Carolina, Daughter of George Cathey (*Source: Neill vs. heirs of George Cathey*).
Children: 1. James Patton - d. in Mississippi-children: William Patton and Sarah Patton,
2. Mary Ann Patton m. Abner Burgin, 3.Ann Catherine Patton m. Hance Alexander McWhorter, 4. George Patton b. 20 Sept. 1786 m. Nancy Patton dau. of Aaron Patton, 5. **Elizabeth Patton** b. 1788 married (1) James Patton (2) David Crockett, 6. Matilda Carolina Patton b. abt. 1795 m. Peter Trosper 7. Rebecca Margaret Patton b. abt. 1800 m. James Edmundson. , 8. Sarah Patton m. William Edmundson. Children may not be in order of birth.

Elizabeth "Betsy" Patton Born: 22 May 1788 Swannanoa, Burke (now Buncombe) Co. N.C.
Died: 31 January 1860 Johnson (*now Hood*) Co., Texas.
Married ca. 1809 (1) **James Patton** Born 1786 – son of Elijah Patton and Margaret Cathey
Died: 23 November 1813 from wounds received at Battle of Talladega – Alabama.

Children of James and Elizabeth Patton: *Photos courtesy of George Patton Family descendants*
(1)George Patton b. 1810 Buncombe Co., N.C. – son of James and Elizabeth Patton - Married: Rhoda McWhorter 27 February 1831 Gibson County, TN George and Rhoda died in Texas.
- 1. James Calvin Patton born 1833, Gibson Co., TN - married Martha Burson died after 1895. Children: Henry J., James W., George W., Robert C., John, C.P, Rhoda A., David P., Samuel Isaac Patton.
    - a. Samuel Isaac Patton b. April 10, 1881 Married: Elah Myrtle Garrett married August 1, 1904–Children: . Elah Bernice, Samuel Burson, Mary Anice, Lois Eleven, Doris Grace, Robert James, Lillian Wathena Patton.
- 2. William W. Patton born 1835 Gibson Co., TN Pvt. Co. K, 15th Texas Calvary CSA – died in battle.
- 3. Robert C. Patton born 1837 Gibson Co., TN- Pvt. Co. C, 10th Texas Infantry Regt. CSA – died in battle.
- 4. Leurges W. Patton born 1839 Gibson Co., TN – Pvt. Co. E 12th Texas Infantry Regt. (Nelson's) CSA – returned from war – remained unmarried
- 5. Benjamin F. Patton born 1841 Gibson Co., TN – Cpl Co. B, McChords Frontier Regt Tx Calvary, CSA – died in battle.

(2) Margaret Ann Patton b. 1811-12 Franklin Co., TN Married: Hance Campbell McWhorter, Also called "Peggy Ann." Children: Elizabeth, John, Irona McWhorter - perhaps more children.
(No photos available for Margaret or her children)

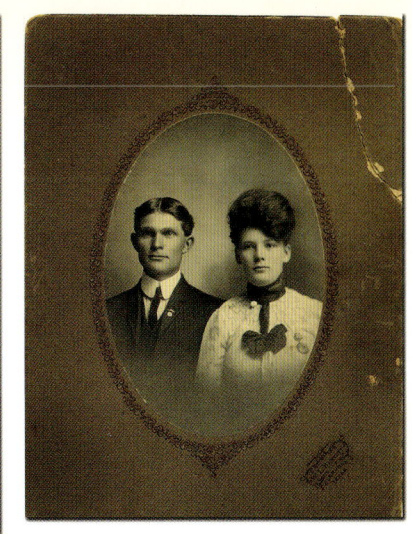

Patton Photographs

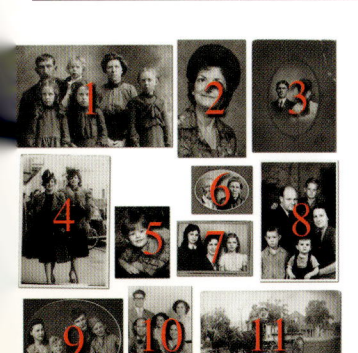

1. George W. Patton Family 2. Doris Grace Patton Browning 3. Sam and Elah Patton - Wedding 4. Anice and Patt Patton in Dallas, Tx 5. Gavin Reese Johnson 6. James Calvin & Martha Burson Patton 7. Marie, Bernice & Betty Vandermere 8. Lois Patton Murray Family 9. Burson Patton and family 10. Robert, Ruth, Bobby, Linda, Ellen, Dauce, Marla Patton 11. Johnny Patton and Sister Rhoda.

Patton-Crockett Family Genealogy

Elizabeth Patton Married **(2) David "Davy" Crocket** ca. August 1815

Children of Elizabeth and David Crockett

(1) Robert Patton Crockett b. 16 September 1816 Franklin Co., TN married Matilda Porter
Children:
- (a) Martha M. Crockett
- (b) John B. Crockett
- (c) Wm. H. H. Crockett
- (d) David L. Crockett
- (e) Bolden A. Crockett
- (f) Mary E. Crockett
- (g) Ashley Crockett and perhaps more children. *Photos of Robert Patton Crockett and family members courtesy of Kenneth Hendricks.*

(2) Rebecca Elvira "Sissy" Crockett b. 25 December 1818 Lawrence Co.TN, moved to Texas with Elizabeth. Married: (1) George Kimbro (2) Rev. James Marion Halford
Children: Five and maybe more
- (a) Martha Matilda Kimbro married: Joseph Anderson Kerr
   - Child: Vivian Evalyn Kerr married: (1) Howard Payne (2) Raymond Carl Oden
      - Child: (i) Ada Virginia Payne Kopf
      - Child: (ii) Raymond Carl Oden, Jr.
- (b) J.C. Kimbro
- (c) J.C. Halford
- (d) David C. Halford
- (e) William L.P.G. Halford

Photos of Rebecca Elvira Crockett descendents courtesy of Ray Oden

(3) Matilda Crockett b. 2 August 1821 Gibson County, TN married(1) Thomas P. Tyson, stayed in Gibson Co., TN. Married (1) Thomas Tyson, (2) James Wilson, (3) Reden Fields.
Children: Four and maybe more
- (a) Mary Tyson
- (b) Candis Tyson
- (c) David Tyson
- (d) Benjamin Tyson

Photo of Matilda courtesy of Joe Bone-Crockett Cabin.
No photos available of her descendants.)

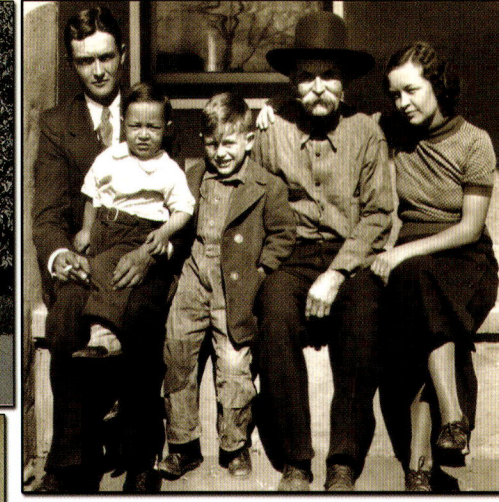

Patton-Crockett Photographs

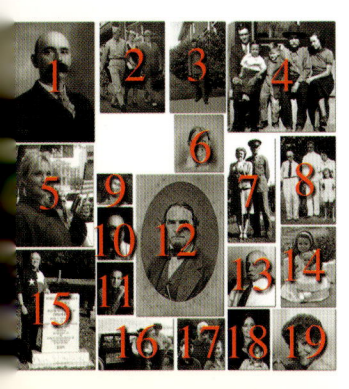

1. Joseph Anderson Kerr - gs of Rebecca Crockett   2. Don King Crockett, Raymond and Gladys Hendricks   3. Private Ken Hendricks   4. Raymond C. Oden, Ray Oden, Jr., Unknown, JosephA.Kerr, VivianKerr   5. Laurie Hendricks Matthews   6. Matilda Crockett - Daughter of Elizabeth and David Crockett   7. Raymond and Gladys Crockett Hendricks   8. Ashley, Cadet David, Helen Crockett Evans & Janet Crockett   9. Carolyn Cotton   10. Jerry Oden   11. Brandon Detherage   12. Robert Crocket - Son of Elizabeth & David Crockett   13. Ashley Crockett   14. Gina & Erin   15. Ray Oden - Acton Cemetery   16. Ken Hendricks and David Crockett   17. Jeff Oden, Justin, Michael   18. Tammy (Detherage) Benedick & Tyler   19. Ada (Payne) Kopf

Crockett-Finley Family Genealogy

David Crockett Born: 17 August 1786 Limestone, Green Co., TN. *(then North Carolina)* Married(1) **Mary "Polly" Finley** Married(2) **Elizabeth "Betsy" Patton** August 1815. Died: 6 March 1836 "Battle of the Alamo," Bexar County, San Antonio, Texas son of John and Rebecca Hawkins Crockett.

David Crockett Married: August 14, 1806 **(1) Margaret "Polly" Finley** Died: March-April 1816 Franklin County, Tennessee daughter of William and Jean Kennedy Finley.

Children of Margaret "Polly" Finley and David Crockett
- **(1) John Wesley Crockett** b. 10 July 1807 married Martha Turner Hamilton
    - Children: Six
        - (a) Mary Elizabeth Crockett Tharpe 1830-1873
        - (b) Robert Hamilton Crockett 1838-1902
        - (c) Alice Ann Crockett Tharpe 1839-1886
        - (d) Petonia Bell Crockett Davis 1847-1897
        - (e) Charles Watrous Crockett 1849-1920
        - (f) Susan M. "Suide" Crockett Tayloe 1852-1885
- **(2) William F. Crockett** b. 25 November 1808 married Clorinda Boyett
    - Children: Two
        - (a) David Crockett
        - (b) William A. Crockett
- **(3) Margaret Finley "Polly" Crockett** 25 Nov. 1812 Crockett – married Wiley Flowers 22 March 1830 Gibson County, Tennessee.
    - Children: Nine
        - (a) Mary Elvira Flowers
        - (b) Harriet Flowers
        - (c) Martha Matilda Flowers
        - (d) Marie Louisa Flowers
        - (e) David Finley Flowers
        - (f) Unnamed twin of David
        - (g) Sarah Ann Flowers
        - (h) Mary Margaret Flowers
        - (i) John Wesley Crockett Flowers

Genealogy of Crockett-Finley Family courtesy of Joy Bland
Official David Crockett Family Website www.genealogy.goahead.org

Crockett-Finley Photographs

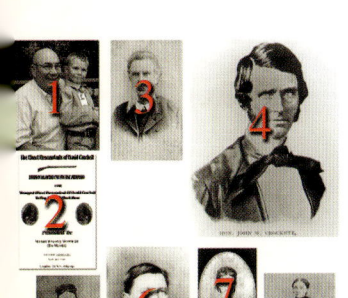

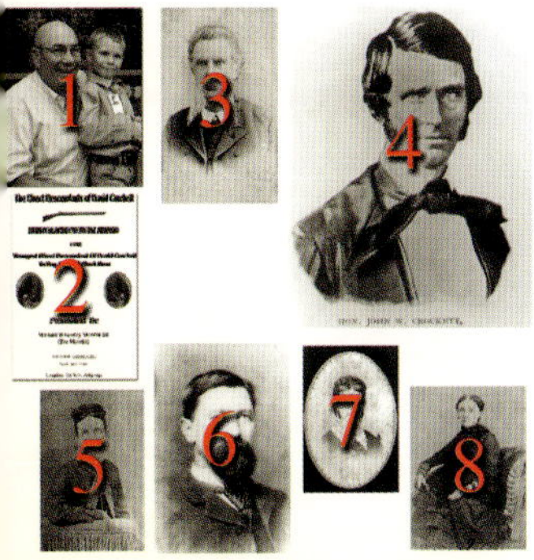

1. Mike & Tre Merritt   2. Hunter Achievement Award for Tre Merritt
3. Robert Hamilton Crockett   4. John W. Crockett
5. Alice Ann Crockett Tharp   6. Charles W. Crockett
7. Mary Elizabeth Crockett Tharp   8. Peytonia Crockett Davis

91

Son of the Author, Tad Browning, has worked as a photographer, videographer and graphics illustrator since 1990. He got his start as an Army Photographer, worked with the Texas Rangers as a forensic photographer and now oversees the audiovisual support for operational testing for the US Army. He has also served as a broadcast journalist in the Texas National Guard since 1997. Including a tour of Iraq in 2005, he has traveled to more than 30 countries doing what he enjoys…capturing life through the eyes of a camera, and of course working with mom.
Email: tadabrowning64@msn.com
www.dfwmediaservices.com

The Author, Helen Ogden Widener, has an ongoing love affair with American History. She is the author of *James MacKay a man to cherish 1761-1822, Irving Centennial Cookbook and family histories 1903-2003* and *Hutchins of Pine Mountain, 200 Years of Migration*. She and her husband James, a retired attorney, live in Irving, Texas and have six children and twelve grandchildren.
Email: hwidener@msn.com
Helen loves to receive questions and comments about her histories.